# YOUR

# RANK

## ADVANCEMENT

## BLUEPRINT

# YOUR
# RANK
## ADVANCEMENT
## BLUEPRINT

HOW TO RANK ADVANCE, AVOID BURNOUT
AND NEVER RUN OUT OF CONTACTS

# R O B
# S P E R R Y

TGON Publishing

# CONTENTS

*"Simplicity is the ultimate sophistication."*

*— Leonardo Da Vinci*

# INTRODUCTION

I can't believe I am starting out my book by admitting one of the most embarrassing things that ever happened to me in network marketing!

Here goes . . . In my fifth month of network marketing, my sales dropped by NINETY-NINE percent!

Yes. You read that right.

In my first month of network marketing, I was still working a full-time job and doing network marketing part-time as a side gig. That first month I received a bonus check of over $15,000. By my fifth month, I had quit my full-time job and made less than $400 in my now full-time network marketing business.

The worst part was that in the fifth month, I worked 80 hours a week and had prematurely quit a 6-figure job running a tennis club. I ended up working much more, making pennies on the dollar. It was more than just embarrassing. It was downright concerning.

How did a guy that had such an epic start get so upside down so very fast?

The simple answer is—I started to complicate the process. The first four months of network marketing I followed the blueprint that my mentor gave me. I kept everything simple and followed the plan. My mentor had told me, "Do what I say, and you will have success." BOOM! I followed his plan and had success.

When the successes kept stacking up month after month, I thought I had figured it out. I started to think it wasn't the process but the player (me) that was hugely successful. I started to get cocky. I thought I could start to play by my own rules. For anyone who has either done this themselves, or watched other people go through this, you probably know what happened. I started to complicate the blueprint.

This is a common problem that I see so many people encounter in network marketing. As people hit new levels of success, they start to complicate systems, processes, and even leadership. I had the blueprint for advancing in the company given to me, but my ego told me I could do it "my way." I got cocky and started to piece together my own tools. Looking back, I can now see that what I was really doing was trying to piece together my success puzzle using five different puzzles!

I made the cardinal mistake in network marketing and complicated the system! I went from being a really successful follower to a really terrible leader of myself. Lucky for me I woke up quick and went back to the blueprint. I realized there was a skill gap that I wasn't able to jump. I knew I needed my mentor's blueprint, some experience, and an intensive course on leadership before I tried that again.

After going through that painful experience myself, I never wanted anyone else to have to struggle like I did. I, of course, went on to create success and crush my network marketing businesses. I know that struggling is part of success, but you can shorten the learning curve if you learn from successful people. I knew when I retired from actively building a network marketing business, I wanted to focus on helping people have success in their network marketing business. I wanted to use my experiences—both good and bad—to help others. I opened my coaching, speaking, and mastermind business where I get to help thousands of people every single year follow the blueprint to success in network marketing. It doesn't matter if they are brand new to the industry or working on creating multiple seven-figure businesses. I have programs, training, and the blueprint for everyone in network marketing.

What about you? How is your network marketing business going? Have you found yourself stuck at the same rank for a few months or even the past year? Maybe you have even gone down a couple of ranks. No need to fear or get frustrated. I will teach you how to use fear and frustration to assist you in your business.

I help people in network marketing in many diverse companies achieve success by rank advancing, having an endless list of contacts, avoiding burnout, and creating a legacy worth living for. Since my time in network marketing, I have helped thousands of people succeed in their own network marketing business with my coaching, books, masterminds, and podcast. As my experience helping people in the network marketing industry grew, I started seeing a pattern. People repeatedly complicate the blueprint. They find themselves stuck or burnt out because they complicated the blueprint. Sounds familiar from my fourth month in the business? As I have been through this myself and watched others complicate the blueprint as well, I realized there had to be a way to teach people to keep it simple. There had to be a format to show them exactly where they are and what they need to do next. With that in mind, I went to work helping my clients and creating the systems and tools that would do exactly that.

I have spent thousands of hours coaching top leaders in the industry and consulting with the very best network marketing companies. I have literally spent my entire career helping others put together the blueprint for success for their companies and businesses. Just this year, I have consulted with top companies to help them create systems for every single person in their company to use. I have helped top leaders create the blueprint for training leaders and showing people how to duplicate that. During all of that, I have been writing down, analyzing, and coming up with the content I am sharing with you in this book. It is time to share the blueprint with everyone! My ultimate goal is to help as many people as I can make money in network marketing. It's that simple! And I know success is possible. I truly think that network marketing is the very best business system on the planet, and I want to help as many people be as successful as they want to be in this industry.

So, are you ready to make money for the first time in network marketing? Or maybe you are ready to make some legacy money in network marketing. Whether you are brand new to this industry, or a seasoned successful professional, this book is for you.

In this book I am going to teach you:

- The Leadership **BLUEPRINT** to generate more profits.

- Keystone habits that will shift your success percentage.

- The process to maximize your time and create a thriving business.

- The formula for spending money in your business.

- How to create a legacy that lasts.

- How to stay relevant in your industry and never fizzle out.

I just gave you six teasers of what is to come in this book. That is just a small sample of what I have created. I am excited to get into this with you and teach you the rest of the blueprint. Everything will be simplified throughout this book with a step-by-step guide to take your network marketing business to an entirely new level. As always, you can find more resources at www.sperrybonus.com.

This book is much more than just a book. It is a study guide to more profits. You will want to read it over and over again. Throughout this book, you will find some sections that are more relevant to where you currently are and other sections that will teach you how to get to the next level. Those will be the sections you will want to focus on the most. You will still want to read the entire book as it will give you a clear future vision of where you want to get to.

Leadership is the ultimate money maker in any business. If you can't lead, you won't make money. Period. There are countless books out there on leading, but leading in network marketing is different from any other industry. I have created three different phases of leadership that correlate directly with how much money you are making in your business, and what type of leader you are. This has never been done before in our industry, and I am confident this book and the phases of leadership are going to help you identify exactly what next skill you need to learn to make more money and become a better leader.

# THE 3 PHASES OF LEADERSHIP
## THE FOUR STAGES

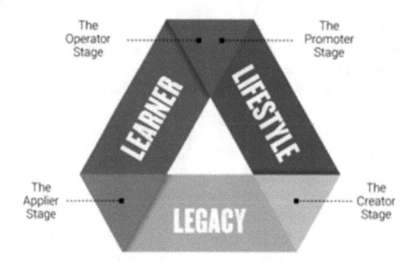

There are three simple phases of leadership that everyone in network marketing goes through. The skills set for each of these phases is very specific and direct. Every single person moves through these phases at different speeds and slight variations. These phases will help you become a leader and will also help you train and create leaders in your business.

You may be thinking, "Why is he talking about leadership?" Because leadership is the key to success. You can't have success in this business without having great leadership. John C. Maxwell said, "A leader is one who knows the way, goes the way, and shows the way." That is exactly the skills you will be learning in this book. In order to rank advance, make money, and accomplish your goals in network marketing, you must learn to lead.

This book is a guide for yourself and your team. You can use it to help assess where you are and the next set of skills you need to work on. The best part is that all of the phases build on one another. Once you have accomplished phase one, you can move on to phase two. The better you get at knowing these skills and phases, the better prepared you will be to lead others through them. This is a system that I use with my own clients and one that I have trained HUGE teams on. The thing I see over and over again is when a simple system is in place, success will follow. The formula has never failed.

I have named these phases of leadership the Learner, Lifestyle, and Legacy phases. As I go through each one, I want you to start identifying what phase you think you are in right now.

This book is segmented into the Three Phases of Leadership. Each of the three sections is a blueprint for success and has massive value. All the sections build off of each other and will intertwine with your leadership style.

## The Learner Phase:

Most of our new team members that sign up in network marketing are here to help themselves and their families survive. Every little bit counts. They see that the 9–5 grind just isn't cutting it for them. Maybe they aren't making the money they want, or maybe the money is there but they are stuck in their corporate offices until all crazy times of nights and weekends. Most people starting out will use the income from network marketing to survive. They come in with little to no experience but a hunger and a hope that this will work for them.

In the learner phase, people have made $0–$10k in total in their network marketing business. During this phase, people are skeptical and fear drives many of their actions. They are desperate to make it

15

work but also fearful of putting themselves out there. This group is in need of great leadership. They need a simple blueprint that they can follow and duplicate. They also need other people to be examples of how easy it is to be successful in network marketing. In this phase, you are learning to be a follower and you are also learning to be a leader to yourself. You have got to start there. Accountability and showing up for yourself are the first leadership skills you will learn. In this phase, you also become a leader to followers. These are people that like you and may like your product, but they aren't entirely bought into the business and doing it themselves. In this phase, you will learn to lead the followers and have the most impact in their lives, which will help you have the most impact in your business.

In PART I, we'll focus on *The Learner Phase* of becoming a leader. Leaders aren't born. In fact, the most successful leaders have had to learn the hard way—with many failures along the path. I'll teach you how to learn from those failures, *apply* the lessons, and use them to *operate* your business. I want to be very clear about this phase. It isn't sexy. This phase is all about building a solid foundation. Foundation work is never sexy. I have all my kids playing tennis right now. They are all in different phases of their skills. My youngest is building the foundational skills to play tennis and he is hating it. He pretends he is SMASHING the ball like his older brother, and he gets frustrated when I make him run drills on holding the racket.

I am going to challenge you to stick with the unsexy in the learning phase. Just like my son is learning to hold the racket. I know from years of being a tennis player and a tennis coach that my son will never smash a ball unless he learns to hold the racket correctly. So, the challenge for you is to build YOUR foundation. Stick with the learning phase and put in the work to build a solid foundation. That way, when you get into the lifestyle and legacy phases, you can SMASH your sexy goals and dreams.

One of the biggest pushbacks I have had while teaching this blueprint is being asked WHY people in the learner phase would need to learn leadership. After all, is someone who is still learning the basics ready to step up and be a leader? The answer is ABSOLUTELY yes! They need training on how to become a leader. They need to KNOW that the basics matter and that they can turn around and teach them to someone else. We need to be training people to be leaders from the very beginning. One of my big leaders I am coaching came and asked me to train a group of new people on his team and I told him I wanted to talk to them about leadership.

He said, "Rob, some of these guys have never even made a sale. That is the wrong topic to be hitting them with." I told my client that it was the exact topic that they needed. In the learning phase of leadership, we are working on building the foundation of skills. We are working on becoming a great follower and knowing what skills you need to work on to become a powerful leader. Build the foundation!

## The Lifestyle Phase:

Once people start making money and paying their bills with their income from network marketing, they start to move into the lifestyle phase. This is the phase where they have moved past survival and are NOW focused on their lifestyle. In this phase, people are making between $10k–$100k annually. They start going on trips, maybe eat out more often and start to create experiences for themselves and their family that they have always dreamed of. The lifestyle phase is where so many dreams become realities for people.

In this phase, you will build on being a leader of followers. This is where you will start to master selling with stories and building your confidence around sharing. You will learn how to create and motivate contacts, guide people through a system, and learn how to duplicate that system over and over again. As you do this, you will move into being a leader of another leader. You will have made such an impact that someone will want to be doing what you are doing, and you will learn to show them how.

Now this is going to sound crazy to some of you, but the lifestyle phase eventually wears out. You go on all the trips, you maybe even move into your dream house, and eventually, you think to yourself, "I wonder what comes next?" I know it sounds crazy, but it is true!

Ask anyone who has been in the lifestyle phase for a bit. I know of a CEO that retired so he could "live the life." He was back to being CEO by the end of the year. The lifestyle phase had worn out. He was ready to create and had a fierce drive. People get tired of the lifestyle phase because they have taken all the trips, lived in the dream house, etc. One of the biggest obstacles in the lifestyle phase of leadership is burnout. They have lived out all the dreams and they are tired! At some point, many lose their PURPOSE in the lifestyle phase.

In PART II, we shift the lens to *The Lifestyle Phase* of leadership. This section incorporates the knowledge you've built upon in the Applier and Operator Stages that we cover in PART I, and shifts the focus to the *Promoter Stage*. This is where you begin to expand your business outside of your own application and operation.

In *The Lifestyle Phase*, we are getting into the meat and potatoes of leadership. I am going to help you with your own personal leadership blueprint that is going to help you stay focused on the goals and move yourself effortlessly into the leadership role in your business as your team starts to grow. We are also going to talk about how you can start your newest team members on this same path and keep it simple for them to grow into leadership.

You may find your level of leadership is higher in one area of your business than in another. That's ok! When I first started in network marketing, I had a high level of leadership in recruiting and low leadership skills in speaking. There will be assessments enabling you to do self-assessment to see where you are at in your leadership in all areas of network marketing. You will never graduate from the phases; you will build upon them. See the phases as groundwork for your leadership that you will always use.

## The Legacy Phase:

In the Legacy Phase, it becomes more about your purpose in life. It becomes about helping other people achieve their goals. It becomes about dying with memories, not dreams. The legacy phase is where you become the person that is known for things that could leave a legacy. In the legacy phase, you are making $100k and beyond. You start to think about impacting your community, and the world. In this phase, you have become a leader of leaders and are now moving into the highest level of leadership . . . mentorship. I want to see more people get to the legacy phase in network marketing, and we will talk more about this in the legacy phase.

Often in this phase, I see people start giving back and really seeing the impact they can make. One of my clients is in the legacy phase and part of our coaching was creating the biggest impact with her money. She started a nonprofit, hired single moms in the community to be on her team and also donates her time and money to the local high school to help every single child that wants to go to college be able to do that. THAT is what the legacy phase is all about.

Every single person in network marketing fits into one of these phases. At each phase, there are skills and lessons to be learned to become the best leader you can be. As you follow the blueprint for each phase you will be able to create more income and move through the phases quicker than you thought. As we go through each phase I will not only tell you the actionable steps to take, but I will also guide you through some of the common obstacles that come up in each phase.

I have seen people stuck in The Learner Phase because they won't invest in mindset coaching. I see people continue to go after lifestyle because they think that will bring them happiness. There is no set time to be in each of the phases. The important thing is that we are aware of them and always seeking to improve ourselves.

When we reach the final section, PART III – *The Legacy Phase*, I am going to teach you to become a legacy leader. This is when we start *The Creator Stage*, effectively employing all the lessons you learned in the previous sections, and actively creating your legacy.

In *The Legacy Phase*, we are going to talk all about legacy and servant leadership. This is where I spend the most time talking to leaders at my leader of leaders masterminds. I have coached the top leaders in the industry on how to continue to have passion and motivation for their ·business as they become the leader of leaders.

It is by far the highest achievement in leadership you can get to, and by far the most fun! The last phase will be by far the longest of them, but all three have equal importance, and you must move through all phases to become the ultimate leader of legacy. Without mastering the first phases you will not be able to fully grasp the final phase.

## Side Effects May Include:

There should be a warning label that comes with network marketing:

WARNING: As you become more successful, you will become a leader of yourself, a leader of followers, and a leader of leaders. Side effects may be personal growth, development, and public speaking. You may also experience a need to share your extraordinary personal story very publicly to inspire others to do the same.

Now that I put this in writing, I see why there is no warning label! Most people wouldn't sign up for that. But these traits do come with the territory of building a team in network marketing. Can you imagine building wealth, success, and leadership all at the same time? That is what network marketing is offering you.

Many come in for the money, but the side effects get them so much more. They get the money, and likewise also get valuable experience, friendships, trips, sales skills, public speaking training and the list could go on and on.

## The Learner Phase $0k–$10

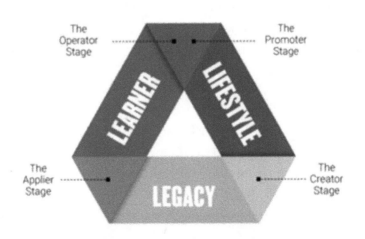

# THE 3 PHASES OF LEADERSHIP
## THE FOUR STAGES

In a recent study, middle-class Americans were asked what they think about on a daily basis.

The number one thing they mentioned was *money*. They thought about how they were going to pay for bills. They thought about how much money they had in their bank account.

They thought about the amount of credit card debt they had.

They also thought about how other people make money, and what other people spend their money on.

One of my good friends in network marketing shared a story with me about when she started her first network marketing business. She said, "I signed up because my friend made ten dollars at her first party selling the product. I was envious of **TEN DOLLARS** because they were threatening to turn off our water and we didn't have the money to keep it on. I was thinking of sitting on a curb and begging, just to keep the water on for my babies. Network marketing felt like the step just before begging."

In the learner phase, people are thinking a lot about money. They are thinking about how ten dollars really could make a huge impact for their families. Some people starting out are focused on making ends meet. Money goes toward keeping the water on, a car payment, or the food bill. People in this phase of network marketing can see the biggest impact in their lives from network marketing, but they are new and therefore have a lot to learn.

When people are in the Learner Phase of network marketing, their skill level is low, but their need for the payoff is high. This is the phase we want to focus on establishing the skills to become an Applier and Operator in their business.

I love this group of people! They are hungry, they are ready, and they have mindset limitations that, once overcome, can unlock amazing potential in them. In the learner phase, people are ready to learn! In this phase I want you to pay close attention to the basics. Learn the basics, become the expert at the basics. This phase is all about learning and DOING.

The biggest misconception about this group is that they are not leaders and that they don't need leadership training. This is false. This is exactly where leadership training needs to begin. They need to learn how to lead themselves and learn to lead by example when doing the basics. In the learning phase, it is crucial to follow the steps and lead by example. When you start something new, like a business, your friends and family are watching to see what happens. You MUST learn to lead and that starts by becoming the best at learning and leading yourself through accountability.

# BLUEPRINT 101

You must remember that you can't compare your chapter one to someone else's chapter twenty-nine. This goes with leadership as well. You can't see a leader that you admire and judge yourself and your leading skills against their chapter twenty-nine. Leadership is not an event. Leadership is an ongoing process. Throughout this book, I will give you the network marketing leadership blueprint.

Leadership isn't a personality trait. Becoming a leader can be taught. Some of the most successful people in life wouldn't have told you that they were natural-born leaders. Being a leader is all skills, mindsets, and strategies that can be learned. I am going to get you prepared for this. I will help you identify where you are in the process of being a leader, what skills you need to learn and gain, and what to watch out for that stifles people from becoming amazing leaders in their organization.

I coach some of the most successful people in this industry. I do training for corporate, and teams. I hold several seven-figure masterminds. One of the biggest gaps I see is the leadership gap. Most successful people in this business know how to work and hustle and are willing to work on themselves, but then they become leaders and they struggle. They don't know how to handle conflict. They struggle to see the motivation for others. They forget how to take care of themselves and maintain boundaries. I watch people suffer imposter syndrome, I see them try and hide or even hire out for their leadership role because they think they don't know how. I watch people complicate the system like I mentioned before to try and compensate for their lack of experience. This ends up having people stall out when they start scaling, trying to duplicate their team, and can ultimately lead to burnout.

Leadership is all about starting with the basic foundations and growing from there. Remember what I said in the introduction; foundations aren't sexy. I want you to commit to doing this work. Commit to the foundation and build it to be rock solid. In my first book, *The Game of Networking*, I talked about how networking can grow your influence and sales. Networking is a basic principle that we were taught in grade school. Think back to the playground. When you wanted to play four squares or see if a boy/girl liked you, you needed to network. If you can learn the basic principles I talked about in *The Game of Networking*, you can build a very successful network of friends and associates. But you must be willing to work on the foundational principles in order to build up from there. I know some adults that STILL have a hard time asking others to hang out, go to dinner, or message them online. This is because they haven't built their foundational principles of networking.

Experts are always made; they are not born. It is the same with leaders. Leaders are made through consistent dedication to the craft of leadership. It takes effort, time, honest feedback, and self-assessment. After decades in this industry and coaching countless leaders, I have come up with the foundation of learning leadership. I will teach you how to start to become the leader you want to be in the future.

That doesn't mean it will be easy. You still are climbing a tall mountain but now you have a path on how to climb that tall mountain. This book will be a guide. My wife and I love to hike whenever we travel. Well, my wife loves to hike, and I love spending time with her. Whenever I tell her about our next trip, she starts researching the biggest mountain we can climb in the area. I have learned something from her. When climbing tall mountains, you must prepare for bad weather, dangerous paths, maybe even wildlife like a cougar or a bear, and many unforeseen obstacles.

This blueprint has mapped out all the obstacles and will give you the clearest path to success and making more money in network marketing. Too often I think that we aren't taught how to be leaders. We are told to build a business without the context of leadership. Follow the blueprint for successful leadership and your business will build itself.

*"The capacity to learn is a gift; the ability to learn is a skill; the willingness to learn is a choice."*

*— Brian Herbert*

# CHAPTER 1

# THE ACTIVE
# LEARNER

At a very young age, Elon Musk knew that it wasn't going to be school that would be the most valuable thing in his life. He knew it was his passion and curiosity that would be his greatest asset. Elon grew up reading two books a day. He took his personal education very seriously and spent hours dedicated to his own personal studies.

Elon said, "Don't confuse schooling with education. I didn't go to Harvard, but the people that work for me did." Elon has always been an avid learner. He has taken learning to the next level in his professional life. Elon has a passion for learning.

Today, Elon Musk is best known as the CEO of Tesla and SpaceX—but way before his success in Silicon Valley, he worked odd jobs to get by. At 17, Musk left his home in South Africa and moved to Canada, where he worked as a farmer, tree cutter, and in the boiler room of a lumber yard.

In network marketing, before you become a leader of leaders, you must first become an actively engaged follower. You must do what Elon Musk has done, and take your personal education in the industry, entrepreneurship, and sales seriously. **A learner is a leader in**

**training.** You must take your role as a learner seriously. All great leaders continue to be learners. This is a skill that will never go unused or be undervalued as you become a leader.

Successful leaders are full-time learners. Knowledge is one of the most priceless assets we can all gain. It is available to everyone, and yet, so many people don't take advantage of it. Most if not all of us have access to the internet. There is a wealth of information at our fingertips, yet so many people stop learning when they become adults.

I was hosting a breakthrough mastermind and there was a young woman in her early twenties. While she was there, she was constantly creating TikToks, and reels on Instagram. Another group of women in their forties was commenting on how they wished they could learn how to do that. The woman in her twenties offered to show them and they declined. "We are too old for that. We are past the age to learn things like that!" These women passed up a golden opportunity to learn FOR FREE from one of the biggest influencers on social media. What a missed opportunity. These women had forgotten the first basic skill of leading . . . You are always a full-time learner. You are never too old, too dumb, or too knowledgeable to learn something new. It doesn't matter what your age or ability level, you should be learning from experience, experts and resources.

Warren Buffet spends five to six hours a day reading newspapers, reports, and books. Warren believes the best investment you can make is the investment in yourself and your learning.

Why do you think the world's smartest people are investing so much of their time in learning?

Warren said, "The more you learn, the more you earn." I agree, as long as you **apply** that learning.

The people stuck have forgotten the importance of being an active learner in their business. They're getting stuck in what I call "Procrastination Development," which is NOT personal development.

Procrastination Development is where you get stuck consuming and never go out and create ANYTHING from what you have learned. You are in the spin cycle of consumption. These people also stop getting on calls with their mentors. They stop furthering their learning in the industry, and personal development takes a back seat because they don't see the value in learning. If this is you, let me be crystal clear, you will not make it to become a high-achieving leader without constant active learning. Leaders make money. You will never become a leader OR make money if you aren't actively learning.

Do not become a broke know-it-all. The broke "know-it-all" is the person that learns every detail and stays in the learning phase. They know everything and do nothing. If you know everything and do nothing, then you earn nothing. You can't watch 1,000 hours of playing the piano and become a great pianist without actually playing the piano. An active learner is learning and applying swiftly and constantly.

Take accountability for your own growth and lead yourself. You can't be arrogant and be in the active learner phase. You have to be willing to lead yourself to development, mentors, and active learning.

Learners are leaders in training. In almost every single professional sport they have training camps. Spring training came around for the NFL one season and one of the head coaches said, "I can always tell who is going to shine during the season. I come early on the first day of spring training and I watch the players make their way into the locker room. Some are hungover, sloppy messes from the off-season. Others are early with their mindset locked and loaded. They have come prepared by not only being physically ready, but one player even showed up with a pen and notebook so he could actively take notes during practice. That is my kind of guy!"

You are constantly in training camp in network marketing. You are learning from your environment and others around you. Ask yourself, "How am I showing up at training camp?" I hope you are the person with a pen and notebook in hand! Active learners take responsibility for their learning, and they come prepared to gain insight that they can act on.

# BEGIN WITH THE END IN MIND

Stephen Covey was one of the greatest leadership experts and always taught: "Begin with the end in mind."

Network marketing is filled with the best leaders on the planet. I have been able to call some of the biggest leaders in network marketing my friends, colleagues, and clients. I always say that leaders aren't born, they are created. So, what has made these people successful in leadership? I have always been fascinated by what makes great leaders and why network marketing is the best training ground for becoming a leader.

Want to know the secret of success and how to create a successful network marketing team? Want to know how to rank advance and continue to make money?

Leadership.

The blueprint for success comes down to learning leadership and becoming the best leader that you can be. I have found that there are stages of leadership in network marketing that no one is talking about!

But what I have found is that the missing piece is that you need to lead from the day you start.

That's right. The day you sign up to have a network marketing company, you are a leader. Throughout this book, I will teach you the level of leadership and how to gain the necessary skills at each level to be the best leader and move into the next phase. Many great leadership books have been written, but we have a HUGE hole in the network marketing industry. We have missed getting specific about what leadership looks like in our industry. Our industry is unique in the fact that we WANT to train other leaders. I was talking to a friend that has been in the corporate world for years. He said he felt like the C-level guys were not willing to train others because they didn't want someone to "take their spot." How sad is that? In network marketing, the highest form of success is having your team outrank and out-earn you! Other books focus on being a leader yourself, but in network marketing, we are focused first on self, second on your newest followers, and third on supporting leaders in your team. The blueprint focuses on leadership skills that you can go through yourself and then turn around and guide your team through.

We are an industry that is built on basic principles, and the best leaders have learned how to do the basics better than anyone else. None of what I am about to teach is unattainable for you. EVERY SINGLE PERSON CAN BE A LEADER. EVERY SINGLE PERSON MUST LEARN TO LEAD FROM THE BEGINNING.

I know some of you may be thinking, "Rob doesn't know me. He doesn't know how shy I am!" I am talking to you! Every single person can be a leader, and I want to teach you how. The key is to break it down with the exact process and blueprint of leadership.

Want more money? Become a better leader.

Want more time? Become a better leader.

Want more happiness? Become a better leader.

John Wooden was the greatest basketball coach of all time. He was obsessed with making his players great and it showed in how he showed up and led. In an interview, he talked about what made him so successful.

John said, *"I personally demonstrated how I wanted players to put on their socks each and every time. Carefully roll the socks down over the toes, ball of the foot, arch, and around the heel, then pull the sock up snug so there will be no wrinkles of any kind. I would then have the players carefully check with their fingers for any folds or creases in the sock, starting at the toes and sliding the hand along the side of and under the foot, smoothing the sock out as the fingers passed over it. I paid special attention to the heel because that is where wrinkles are most likely.*

*I would watch as the player smoothed the sock under and along the heel. I wanted it done conscientiously, not quickly or casually. I wanted absolutely no folds, wrinkles, or creases of any kind on the sock. Then we would proceed to the other foot and do the same."*

Coach Wooden is a great example of one of the principles I teach people about becoming successful at whatever they are doing. Successful people just do the basics better.

It doesn't matter whether you are learning how to be the most successful basketball coach of all time OR a successful leader in network marketing; you must be committed to learning the basics better.

Successful people just do the basics better. Successful leaders teach others how to do the basics better and duplicate that teaching over and over again.

I was able to have more success in my first month working part time in network marketing than I had in my fifth month working full time in network marketing. Why? My first month I had a full-time job that I was working forty-five hours a week and my network marketing job was my side hustle. I had never done network marketing. I had zero experience, but I was able to absolutely smash it. I generated over $45,000 in sales and received a paycheck for over $15,000.

Fast forward to my fifth month. I had more experience, I had transitioned to network marketing full time, and it was my entire focus. I had given up watching TV. I focused on personal development. My knowledge was through the roof compared to month one on both the products and industry. But my check had gotten all the way down to less than $400 for the month—despite working over 80 hours a week. What has changed?

Shouldn't my paycheck be growing, not lowering?

I had to discover for myself that successful people do the basics better. I was failing because I wasn't doing the basics and I was trying to fill in the voids of doing the basics with arrogance.

I started "vomiting" facts all over everybody—giving them all the latest and greatest statistics on why the company was so great and why the products were so incredible. I told them all about the compensation plan in detail and why it was so great. I gave them so much information that it took away from the simplicity, the passion, and the excitement. It masked the vision and turned the energy level way down. I was the living example of "facts tell, stories sell." I was selling nothing because I was feeling like I was over the basics and had moved into "leadership" by telling people what to do!

My insecurities began to intensify, and instead of keeping it simple, I tried to get rid of the insecurities by complicating it for everyone—myself included. This happens for everyone, as our insecurities intensify, we start to talk more, and try to fill in our lack. We start to complicate it by showing people that we know what we are talking about. Successful people do the basics better. It truly is as simple as that. They don't overcomplicate a sale by letting their ego do the talking. They keep it simple; they keep it basic, and they go out and do it over and over again. Jim Rohn said it best: "There is power in brevity." Let's use Jesus Christ as an example. He said, "Come follow me." He didn't say come follow because . . . followed by some long, crazy story. The more confident and secure you are, the more you keep it brief and simple.

# Keystone Habits

One of the things that I see active learners do is create KEYSTONE HABITS. A keystone habit is a base habit that you will commit to and do no matter what. Think about brushing your teeth or washing your face. For many people, these two habits are keystone habits. They will brush their teeth at night no matter what time they go to bed and where they are. We were once on a Lake Powell trip and one of our friends forgot their toothbrush. He spent the entire trip brushing his teeth with his finger three times a day. Brushing his teeth was a keystone habit that he wasn't willing to quit doing for anything!

Keystone habits are HUGE when you are becoming an active learner. You need to think for yourself what your keystone habits in your business are going to be. Let me be clear, these habits must be done—NO MATTER WHAT! There are very few emergencies that warrant getting out of keystone habits.

When I started this business, I created personal and business keystone habits. Personal development was going to be a keystone habit. Since I set that habit, I haven't missed a day of personal development in fourteen years. I have been through A LOT in fourteen years, but the keystone habits have always been hit. Some days that personal development was only five minutes, but that is OK! I still kept that promise to myself and made the keystone habit part of my day.

One of my clients decided that physical exercise was a keystone habit for himself. He set the habit and decided he would never go a day without missing fifteen minutes of exercise. One of his kids ended up in the hospital. It turned his whole family's life upside down. He and his wife would take turns to spend time in the ICU with their daughter. My client told me, "This was the hardest part of my life. I didn't know if I was going to lose my little girl. I spent hours sitting in a chair next to her bedside. But, every single day, I would set my alarm and for fifteen minutes in her room, I would do a workout. Sit-ups, planks, squats, whatever I could do to hit the keystone habit. As hard as that was, that keystone habit helped keep me sane and active during that trying time." Lucky for my client, his little girl is doing amazing.

That is a pretty extreme case of keeping keystone habits, and I wanted to share it here, because you really can keep keystone habits through so much adversity. So often people get knocked off course by the smallest things.

I have heard things like holidays, weather, or even the phases of the moon as top excuses why people don't do their keystone habits. In this phase of leadership, you are learning to keep promises to yourself and show up and do what you say you are going to do. Keystone habits will help you do that. You have got to create a minimum and non-negotiable on your very worst week when you don't feel like it, when you're sick and when you're unmotivated. How many new contacts are you going to make? We could give several examples of some good minimums for business, then your standard goal is the one that you are hoping to do every week.

Think about your business. What is your keystone habit minimum around new contacts made on a daily or weekly basis? What could you do in your best week? What about your worst week?

In future chapters, we are going to talk about building on your keystone habits so you can start to create great momentum and even ignite your business through your keystone habits. But for now, create the baseline keystone habits in your business. What will you commit to daily, weekly, and monthly that you can do and sustain through anything?

Here are the top FIVE keystone habits that every single person in the learning phase of network marketing needs to start in their lives.

1 - Spend at least 30 minutes in your "Daily Methods of Operation." These are also known as DMOs. These are actions that you are taking to make money.

2 - Thirty minutes of personal development. You can read or listen to a book, watch YouTube, take a course, etc. This time needs to be focused specifically on you and the areas of growth in your own life that you would like to focus on.

3 - Speak to five new people a week. Yep, you read that correctly. Every single week you should be reaching out to at least five new people. This could be via social media, in person, or even at your kid's sporting events. Meet new people and learn to connect with them WITHOUT pitching. Genuinely connect with others. If you need help in this area, use your personal development time to read my book *The Game of Networking.*

4 - One hour a week dedicated to the relationships closest to you. This could be a spouse, kids, best friend, or neighbors. It is so important as we build businesses that we don't get too busy or forget those relationships that mean the most to us. Turn off your phone and really connect with the people you love.

5 - Spend 30 minutes a day on taking care of your body. One of the best things I have done for myself over the years is being meticulous with how I take care of myself. Your body is one of your biggest assets and if you don't take care of it, you will find yourself really broken, really fast. Spend this time going for a walk, meal prepping, or whatever else feels like taking care of your body to you.

I just gave you the five top keystone habits that will have the biggest impact in your life. You have one hundred and sixty-eight hours in a week. These keystone habits will take you around fourteen hours. I promise you if you invest the time, your investment will pay off hugely!

Newsflash! The biggest obstacle that people face creating when sticking to keystone habits is accountability. Your best accountability is going to come from yourself. You must be willing to hold yourself accountable and set expectations that you are willing to continue to come back to. This takes preparation and commitment. In order to lead others, you must work on first leading yourself. No one is going to hold your hand and do things for you. You have to be willing to be accountable to yourself. How you show up matters! I want to tell you the biggest mistake that people make with self-accountability. They use accountability to beat themselves up and allow negative self-talk. Don't be that person! Accountability isn't a bullying session with yourself. It is a time to stick to the facts and use them to adjust what needs to be adjusted and get back in there.

For example, if I set the goal to do the five keystone habits, and during my accountability check-in I see that I have done all of them except for the one hour a week with my family, I need to be accountable. I look and ask myself a couple of questions.

1 - What is the excuse I am telling myself as to why I didn't do that?

2 - Is it valid? Why or why not?

3 - What can I do differently next week to make sure this happens?

Simple. No beating myself up. No feeling terrible and calling myself all sorts of names. I ask questions to see where I am at and how I can be even better next week.

Self-accountability is all part of the mindset and personal development work. Do you believe that you will level-up from your learning? Do you have a belief that you are surrounding yourself as you meet other people that don't serve you? If the answer is yes, don't beat yourself up. Be accountable. See where your weakness is and work to change it.

You can't lead an army if you can't lead yourself. Lead yourself by being accountable to your growth and development. Be the leader of one by being your biggest fan, cheerleader, coach, and accountability partner.

In airplanes, the flight attendants instruct you to put on your own oxygen masks just as you must learn to put your mask on first before you help others. That is the exact same concept in leadership. You have got to become an active learner first before you help anyone else thrive. This goes in all areas of your life.

People sometimes feel like this is completely selfish. They want to go out and try to help everyone. But they can't even help themselves! Learn to be an active learner for yourself. Don't spend all of your time focused on other people that you neglect yourself.

I was coaching a leader who was completely burnt out. She was thinking of quitting network marketing because of the complete exhaustion she was experiencing. I asked her when the last time was that she spent time on her own learning and growth and not on catering to other people's needs. She sat there silent for a couple of minutes. "I don't think I have done that since the first year of my business. I go to a lot of training, but I am always focused on learning for other people and not myself."

She had run out of oxygen in her business because she hadn't taken the time to put her own oxygen mask on first. You will never help anyone else when you are suffocating in your business. Many times, focusing on helping others when you haven't helped yourself is a distraction you create to avoid the difficult progress of YOU becoming better.

Think back to Elon Musk and Warren Buffet. They have not only put on their own oxygen masks but then also turned around and figured out how to make money showing other people how to do it or creating better masks themselves! THAT is being an active learner. Taking your own personal learning seriously. Set up time in your business that you are actively learning for yourself.

When I started in this industry I was obsessed with learning. I wanted to learn the process of sponsoring and duplication, but I also wanted to learn what the best leaders were doing. I paid attention and learned how they were dressing, how they presented in front of thousands of people. I was actively learning all about the business and about how the top leaders acted, looked, and sounded.

I was starting to envision myself and what I could become. I started to believe that I could be a top leader. I realized early on that it wasn't "fake it till you make it." That never works! I learned that it was actually a process of "Act as if . . . to become." This is important to fully understand so pay close attention.

I hear people all of the time saying, "But Rob, I will never be like that leader." "Rob I could never do it that way." They are not ACTING as if. They are waiting for someone or something to come along and tell them it is ok. You can't do that when you are actively learning. You must act as if—so that you CAN become in the future.

I started thinking, "How would the highest-level leaders act? How would they talk? How would they speak?" I observed the best and biggest leaders. I would ask questions of my mentors and people I looked up to. After I actively listened and learned, I would then turn around and think about myself as that powerhouse leader. I had to think about how the bold version of myself would show up. How would I act, how would I talk, how would I speak? What would my posture and swag be if I was in the confident leader energy? How would that MILLION-dollar version of you ACT? Becoming the best version of you, all begins with acting as if you were that person already.

In my mind, I knew I had to become the leader first in my mind. I had to act as if, so that then my actions would follow and actually create the result of that huge rank I was going after. Active learners that are becoming great leaders all work on becoming first, and having the results follow.

# Future Self Day

Have you ever wondered how people go from believing that something is possible to actually making it happen? I know that for a long time, I was stuck with where I was and seeing where I wanted to go. I couldn't figure out how to show up in the full belief that I was a millionaire before I had any evidence that it was true. Here is an exercise you can try that I learned from one of my good friends Carrie Marshall. Carrie is a master goal coach who helps people achieve their biggest goals. She loves helping her clients bridge the gap from belief to reality by doing an exercise called the "Future Self Day."

## Here is how it works:

Find a time on the calendar and schedule a Future Self Day. This is the day that you will spend acting as if you are already that successful leader of leaders. You are making the type of money you want and living the life you want to lead. It is fascinating how this exercise will help you learn some key things you may need to start doing or stop doing to become the future you.

I introduced my Future Self Day to one of my clients and she had a lot of objections. "I don't have any clothes that my future self would wear. I still have to go into my full-time job, and so I can't have the schedule my future self would be able to have." It's not about making all the details match up. It is about showing up in a different frame of mind. Show up to your full-time job in the best dress that you own. Don't complain during the day but find the leader's energy that maybe you usually don't have at your work. Take the time in the car ride home to listen to a motivational talk instead of listening to music. Do everything you can on your Future Self Days to show yourself what is possible, even if the details don't fit. This is one of the best learning exercises I watch clients get to experience.

I remember when I was building my first network marketing business, I had this huge goal. I wanted to hit a particular rank. It was the highest-level rank in the company that usually took people five or more years to hit in the multi-billion dollar company. My goal was to hit this rank within five months.

I was relentless in my pursuit of hitting the rank. The five-month mark came along, and I didn't hit it. Six months came and went, and I didn't hit it yet. My mentor became worried and thought I would get discouraged by not hitting my goal. But he didn't know how much active learning I was putting towards my future self. I was working hard on my mindset every single day, and so in my mind, I still felt like I had accomplished the goal. I was putting in the time; I was putting in the effort. I had a complete belief that I was getting there.

Many other people in the company knew about my goal, and by month seven these people were checking in with me and asking if I was disappointed because I still hadn't hit the rank. Word had gotten out that I was driven and going for the huge goal. More and more people checked in with this "tough break" attitude towards me. They expected me to be ashamed and licking my wounds.

I could have been frustrated in a negative way and I could have gotten all whiny and blamed other people. I could have focused on the problems and sulked about not having gotten what I wanted. But where does that lead? That leads to a victimized place like I talked about in *The Game of Conquering*. It leads to being the victim of our own lives.

I chose to be the conqueror. I chose to take 100 percent ownership when I didn't hit my goal. YES, I was mad, but not at the world, not at other people. I was mad and driven in a positive way. It helped fuel my actions to keep pushing. It helped me get even more passionate about actively learning. I had declared to the world what I wanted, and I was putting in the time and the effort. I knew it was inevitable that I would earn it, but it hadn't happened yet. That is the way of an active learner. That is being a learner in training. That is the foundation of a leader!

Compensation always catches up to skill set and effort, but it's almost always massively delayed. This is a quote I came up with that would give me perspective. I knew I was doing the work. I was learning and growing with my skill set and effort. I just needed to wait for my compensation to catch up to me! By month eight of not hitting the rank, I started to slide into the victim and blame mode. I was mad because I just felt like I had become that high-level rank in my mind. I had lost the learner and had become entitled. How many of you have found yourself here? Stop and think about this. Remember the excitement in the beginning? When did that wear off? When did you start to feel entitled to your dreams? This is the result of dropping off being a learner. This is what happens when we stop our active pursuit of knowledge and experience.

Going into month nine I recognized the entitlement I was feeling. I had to be completely honest with myself and see where I stopped taking ownership of my learning. I figured out that I had stopped doing Future Self Days. I had stopped learning and asking questions. I had stopped being honest with myself about where I was and started to only think about where I should be.

I sat myself down and did a reset. I committed again to becoming an active learner. I committed again to my value of "always learning" and really thought about what else I could learn. I wanted to know what else was missing that I could continue to learn.

This is a skill that all leaders learn to do. They are always actively learning. They never think anything should be handed to them just because they did the work. Leaders are active learners for the sake of curiosity, knowledge, and experience. Compensation will catch up! When I got back into active learning mode in month nine, magic happened.

I hit that rank and kept hitting it. I accomplished my goal faster than anyone in the company had that year. That was in a company that had a million distributors, and I did it through active learning.

The craziest part is that it wasn't as big of a celebration as I thought because, in my mind, I had expected it. In my mind, I had already hit it, it just took time for the compensation and reality to catch up. When I got back into active learner mode and continued to work on becoming, it became inevitable that I would hit it and move beyond that rank to the next level of leadership.

When the awards at the company retreat came out later that year, they announced my rank and that I hit it faster than anyone else. Once again, I was a bit surprised that it really wasn't the acknowledgment that mattered to me. I was so proud of the person I had become. I was proud that I had found the secret to success, and that it came when I was focusing on actively learning.

Sure, it took me twice as long as I would have hoped, but again, that's something that John Maxwell teaches. Everything worthwhile is always harder than we think it's going to be. That's not just network marketing that's everything in life, everything worthwhile is always harder than we think it's going to be. And it was another learning lesson for me that that is 100% true.

# LALA

Want to know the best way that you can become a leader TODAY? I call it the LALA approach. Anytime you are going to be doing training, personal development, or learning something new, you can use this approach. The objective is to be an active learner who shows up and doesn't stay in "learner mode" for too long.

## LALA means: Listen, Apply, Learn, Action.

Let's break it down. As you are doing new things you will need to LISTEN to what is being said. Most network marketing companies have systems in place for their company. Most of your uplines or mentors will be teaching you these systems. As you learn from your mentor, I want you to apply LALA. Listen intently and pay attention to what is being said. Don't ask questions just to sound smart, LISTEN first!

Next, APPLY what you are listening to. Most people jump to learning, but first, you must apply by writing notes, thinking about how the message applies to you. I see people jump to learning without stopping and thinking for themselves! Many people have it backwards. Listen, then apply. Ask yourself one question as you listen, "How does this apply to me?" Ask that question as often as needed.

Now, we can LEARN. You can spend time learning because you now know how it applies to you. You are actively engaged in listening, applying and learning. And finally, take Action. This is the step that most people forget. They spin in the learning cycle and never take action. ACTION is key in the LALA approach. Once you have listened, applied, and learned, it is time to take action.

This business is built on taking action. And I am not talking about one-and-done action. I am talking about daily action in your business. Don't be the person that gets sucked into the personal development black hole. If you're the person who knows everything and does nothing, you earn absolutely nothing. Don't misinterpret PD (personal development) as procrastination development. Take action!

One of my friends likes to say, "YOU can tell me all day how to do something, but can you show me?" Ralph Waldo Emerson said it best, "What you do speaks so loudly I cannot hear what you say."

Take action and implement what you're learning right away. Yes, it does get repetitive, but that's the way that we learn and the way we make money. So, we need to make sure that we're constantly listening, applying, learning, and taking action. At my mastermind events for people that are nearing a breakthrough, I have them create an entire page of executables. These are things that they are going to go home and actually execute. I don't care if they have just gotten the best information in the world, if we're not actually executing it means absolutely nothing.

The saddest thing to me is someone that has invested in being at the mastermind and they have gotten so much wisdom and value from being there. When I check in with them six months later and they haven't done anything with that knowledge I get bummed for them. You must actively learn AND go out and quickly apply!

## What you can do right now to continue being an active learner:

- Watch company training (with a pen and notebook!). - Schedule a time to talk with your upline.

- Whenever you take notes, create a separate section or even notebook that has your executables. You can continually update the priority of those executables, but you should always have your executables written down in order of priority. FOCUS!

- Use the LALA approach to learning new things.

- Watch my training on belief found on www.sperrybonus.com

- Create a learning plan for the next three months. Actively engage in the plan. Learn. Take action. Assess. Adjust. Repeat.

- Do a self-assessment. Where are you lacking knowledge?

- Set up five KEYSTONE habits to be an active learner. These are NO MATTER WHAT habits that you are willing to commit to every single day. Keep promises to yourself. PERIOD.

- Write down what your future self will be. How will they act, think, look, and what will they be doing? Schedule Future Self Days at least once a month.

*"I've missed more than 9,000 shots in my career. I've lost more than 300 games. 26 times I've been trusted to take the game winning shot and I have missed. I've failed over and over again in my life."*

*— Michael Jordan*

CHAPTER 2

# THE FAILING
# LEARNER

Elvis Presley didn't start out with fame and fortune. He grew up so poor that his family couldn't afford rent and so they would live in a boarding house with his family where the kids could work for their room and board. As Elvis grew up, he always loved to sing and imagined himself being able to sing in front of an audience. He would go and try out for any band, club or audition he could find, but time and again he was rejected, and told he would never amount to anything. Once, during an audition, he was even told to go back to his day job of driving trucks because that was the best he would ever do in his life.

No matter how disheartened he would get, Elvis was the mate student of music. He would take notes from the rejections, practice, and then go back and audition again. He eventually performed "That's All Right" which caught the attention of the right people in the music industry. The rest is music history. Elvis is one of the most listened to and celebrated singers of all time. He has sold billions of records worldwide and is still a household name.

What most people forget about Elvis Presley is that the failures didn't stop after he became a world-famous superstar. He continued to fail his way to success throughout his career. In 1956, Elvis performed at his first show in Las Vegas. He was always trying new things and wanted to push himself both with his look and sound. It confused the audience so much that the show was cut short, and he was told that he would never perform again in Las Vegas unless he would give the audience, "the Elvis they all love."

Elvis is still to this day seen as the King of Vegas. Imagine that! The King of Vegas was once kicked off the stage of Vegas! Here is the best part. He didn't go back to the Elvis that everyone loved. He continued to progress and push himself and his music. He was willing to fail and go back out and try again. He later created and performed in the most sought-after show in Las Vegas for years. Elvis can teach us so much about how to become a leader through failure.

# Failure = Growth

Someone that has a growth mindset has a failing attitude. A failing attitude doesn't mean that you are always thinking about failing. It means they are WILLING to fail, and you see failure as feedback and learning experience.

As a leader, your next level of growth is always going to come from learning new things. You can't stay stagnant as a leader. You must be willing to try new things and be willing to fail over and over again. No one gets to learn through perfection. Ever. As I watch new leaders scale, I always watch and coach them on their mindset around failure. I know that if someone is terrified of failure, they are going to stall out in progression.

To become a leader that can lead others, you must be willing to fail. Failure won't stop at the beginning of your career either. You must be willing to fail over and over again for the REST of your career. Failure is not an option; it is a requirement of all great leaders. Failure is where growth and learning happen.

One huge mistake that I see new leaders in network marketing make is that they think they can't or shouldn't fail. They have a belief that they "should" know how to do something (or everything!).

At some point, adults decided that failures shouldn't happen anymore. We tell ourselves that if we fail, it means that we aren't valuable. If an entrepreneur told you they had never failed, they probably aren't entrepreneurs! Every single successful entrepreneur I know fails a lot and often. That is because they are taking big risks, trying new things, and taking massive action. They have also upped their chances of having HUGE successes.

Many of us have a skewed way of looking at failure. As I was interviewing and researching 'fear' for my book The Game of Conquering, I found that one of the biggest fears that adults face is the fear of judgment which is the mother of all fears. Every nonphysical fear we face stems from the fear of judgment. When we got a more specific one, the top fears mentioned from the fear of judgment was the fear of failure. In the *Game of Conquering,* I spoke in depth about the fear of failure because it is something that holds people back time and time again. Failure is meant to teach. Failure is where ultimate learning can happen.

## Learning to Fail

My mentor has now made over $30 million in the network marketing profession. He is not only a complete and total legend, but he has one of the strongest personalities I have ever met in my life. I knew him for several years before I started in network marketing. I was coaching his kids in tennis. At that time, I didn't even know that he was part of network marketing because he had done so well and was completely retired. But once a network marketer ALWAYS a network marketer. He was getting the itch to get back in the business because he saw people like myself that could greatly benefit from the industry and his expertise.

When he decided to come out of retirement, I began to work with him, and I had so many fears! I was completely scared. I talked about many of these fears in my book, *The Game of Conquering*, but there was one particular story that I wanted to share with you.

I was on my very first conference call with several thousands of people. I had only been in the business for about six weeks, and my mentor wanted me to speak on this big conference call. Of course, I was nervous and excited all at the same time. I got on and did what I thought was a pretty great job. At the very end of the call, I felt amazing, and I thought I had done so well.

My mentor asked me one question, "On a scale of one to ten, how do you think you did?" I wanted to seem modest, so I told him I thought I was a seven.

He paused and stayed quiet for a bit. He said, "On a scale of one to ten you were a three."

Before I could say anything, he said, "NO, that's not right. I am just trying to be nice. You were a one."

He then went on to tell me that I was monotonous, boring, and to top it all off he said, "You sounded like you were at your father's funeral."

He went silent and waited for my response. I still remember where I was when I had this conversation with my mentor. I was on the top floor of our townhome right in between my kids' bedrooms and the bathroom. I fell to the ground, laughing as loud as anyone could. And my mentor was stunned, "Rob . . . Are you laughing?!"

Between wiping my tears and trying to catch my breath in between the laughs I told him I was laughing.

He said, "Wow, you are going to be great at this business. If you already have the ability to handle this type of critique. Then you are going to be an incredible learner. You are going to be able to take your business to an entirely new level, and I can tell you're going to become one of the legends in this industry."

The reason I wanted to share this story with you is that I wanted to illustrate that I came into this business as a one. That's right! A one! I still smile at this. It wasn't coming in with an incredible skill set that made me succeed. It was my ability to be able to learn, and my willingness to fail. I knew I could learn from the failure, and it didn't bother me being a "one." I knew in order to have more success I just needed to FAIL faster and learn from each particular failure.

## Fail Fast.

## Fail Forward.

## Fail for a Reason.

## Fail from Where You Are

Allow yourself to be where you are at. You don't have to be anyone different to do this business. You can start where you are and know that improvement, development, and progression are in your future. This goes back to the keystone habits and being accountable. Set yourself up for trying something new, big, and scary that you haven't done before by being 100 percent accountable to yourself. What went well? What needs improvement? What should you never do again?

The ability to learn is the greatest ability you can possess. You can learn how to speak in front of thousands. You can learn how to sell.

You can learn to lead. You can learn to make friends as an adult. If you don't know how to learn, you are stuck forever. You will never be able to transition into the next stages that I talk about in this book if you do not take your learning seriously. I promise you that you will want to get to the next stages of your self-development, because they are the stages of leadership that will pay off the most.

You must be willing to learn. With learning comes failure. No one learned to walk without falling down. We are set up from the time we are born to learn by failure. Somewhere along the road, we switch and start to say things like, "Failure is not an option." For some people this may be a motivating tagline, but why would we not let failure be an option?

To be an active learner, you must be actively failing and learning from the failure. Just like I did with my first conference speaking. There is a HUGE difference between being a person that is failing and a person that is quitting. If I were to switch the tag line up, I would say, "Quitting is not an option." Failure is part of the process.

When my mentor told me I was a "one" I didn't let that be my excuse to quit. I let it motivate me. After I stopped laughing, I listened. I learned. I got feedback. I went back out and tried over and over again. I am still learning how to speak in front of audiences. With all my expertise and experience, I still ask for feedback and learn how to make it even better. You see you think about your failures as just that ... failures but they can be so much more.

Your failures are such an important part of your story. Your struggles give you perspective. Your struggles, if you overcome them, help to connect you with your teams. When you struggle, tell yourself this, "This is going to be such an important part of my story to share someday."

## Get Comfortable with Failure

I will take someone who is new, hungry to learn, and willing to fail any day over someone that has raw talent and is lazy. We look at people and think, "If only I had the type of talent they had. If only I was as good as they are." But what we don't understand is that grit and resilience will get you through your bad day, bad week, or bad month. If you don't have the mentality of a failing learner, YOU ARE DONE. A new study of more than 11,000 West Point cadets over 10 years found that "grit" was the most important trait for success—beating out brains and brawn.

Researchers—who defined "grit" as "passion and perseverance for long-term goals of personal significance"—said cadets who displayed that special quality were more successful during the challenging four-year military academy that begins with "Beast Barracks," a notoriously brutal six-week basic training program.

"Cognitive and physical abilities each enable progress toward goals in their respective domains," the study said. "In contrast, grit seems to enable individuals to keep going when the going gets tough."

Think about your mindset around failing. Where are you letting your fear of failure stand in your way? Where are you telling yourself that failure is not an option? When are you afraid of failing in front of your mentor, family, or friends? So what if you get rejected from friends and family. So what if someone chooses to quit your team and do something outside of network marketing. It definitely hurts but stop taking everything so personal. Your perspective on your so-called trials is everything. You choose what story you are going to tell yourself based on every single experience. You decide if you are going to look at each experience as one that teaches and empowers you or if you are going to look at each experience as an excuse to not pursue your dreams. Imagine this scenario for a minute. When your server at a restaurant offers you coffee and you say no, is that server offended? No, of course not. When it comes to network marketing, we take every 'no' so personally. Some people just don't want a drink of coffee, just like some won't ever have any interest in your business. Both are ok. Be the server!

Being a leader means failing yourself and watching your team fail over and over again. If you are not able to change your mindset about failure, you will struggle to lead a team. There is only one way to the top, and it is the trail that is sprinkled with failure. Your failure is your feedback. Your mess is your message if you are willing to overcome it. Be willing to change your attitude around failing and start to see it as an opportunity to grow, learn, and then turn around and use it to connect and inspire others. You can be a failing leader; you can't be a quitting leader.

I had several huge failures while building my network marketing business. We have all had people quit, but I remember this particular time where I had recruited these amazing people to build, and out of nowhere they all quit. People of course make their own decisions, and I can't decide if they succeed or quit, but when this group of leaders quit, I had to take accountability and ask myself, "How did I contribute to them quitting?" Instead of sulking about it and hiding from it, I had to learn from it, adjust what I was doing, and finally make my mess my message.

First, I sat down and learned everything I could for myself to make sure it would never happen again. Second, I thought about how I could use it to help train my clients and leaders and help everyone out. This is what being a failing leader looks like! We learn from our own mistakes and then we turn around and help others. Failure is feedback! I learned from this particular experience that I was micromanaging people. I was used to being a leader of followers, but NOT used to being a leader of leaders. I hadn't gained the skills to truly motivate and empower others who were ready to run! I was able to identify my weakness and went out and learned how to be a leader of leaders.

At one of my mastermind events, I was speaking about using failure as feedback and using your own failures as your message to teach your team. A man at the event raised his hand and said, "This is embarrassing to say, but I have never once let my team know of my failures. I was taught that failure is weak, it shows people that you could be easily taken out." This man was afraid to be seen as weak to his team, so he had held back the biggest part of his message.

Funny enough, this same man was having a difficult time connecting to his team. He said that a couple of his people had told him he wasn't approachable and that they had a hard time coming to him with their problems.

I spoke with him at the end of the event, and we did some deep-dive coaching into what was coming up for him around failure and his mindset. Three months later he called me and said he had a major breakthrough with the team.

When we had coached together, he saw that he was embarrassed to admit failure because he was taught about failure being something bad about a person. He saw people in his life put to the side and shunned when they had failed. This pattern was showing up in his team. When he was able to identify it, he was able to see how this one belief about failure from the time he was a kid was having an impact on his business.

After he worked through that, we worked on making his failure his feedback, and also on making the *mess the message*. He had done a team call and had shared his messes and failures with the leaders on his team. It was the hardest call he had ever done, but the payoff was

HUGE! The team started to open up, they got over roadblocks that had held them back, and they started to collaborate together. They started to see him as a leader to whom they could relate. A failing leader knows the value of sharing the failures with their team.

A leader shares them, not to tell the team they are a screwup, or that they are a hot mess! A leader shares failures to help the team connect and learn. A leader shares to inspire and motivate. At this point in leadership, you are new and may be thinking, "I don't have those big stories of success to share." Perfect! People want to connect with the real authentic you. They don't need a Cinderella story to be motivated. They need you.

One of my coaching clients started network marketing because her son had disabilities that require lots of doctor's appointments. She said that she had been fired from her past two jobs because she missed so much work. She shared her story on social media the first week she signed up. She hadn't figured it out, She hadn't made millions of dollars, she made a post that said, "Hey, y'all! As you know my son has been in and out of the hospital and doctor's visits for some time. Unfortunately, that means I haven't been able to find a job that will let me take that much time off work. I have been laid off from my last two jobs. It has been hard, but I am determined to find something that works for my family."

The outpouring of support and love was there from everyone that saw it. She told me that the most mind-blowing thing was how many other parents reached out and said that they were in the same boat. They told her if she figured out how to make something work to let them know. She now leads a team mostly made up of parents that have kids with disabilities. At the time of the post, she was sharing what was authentic to her and her life. You need to do the same! Don't wait until you hit some crazy number or rank advance. Share yourself and your story and watch what can happen.

## Grit and Perseverance

Part of being a failing learner is having grit and perseverance. I always say you must marry the process and date the results. If you truly have the grit, it is a combination of having both that incredible passion and also having the perseverance to go through the struggles and tough times. You have to have both. I have seen it all too often. Some very talented people have joined network marketing, and they have the talent and passion. But they lack grit and perseverance, and they end up failing and quitting. They can't make it through that bad day, bad week, and bad month. They end up quitting. If you can—focus on grit in this learning phase and you can marry the process and divorce the results.

If you have been in network marketing for even less than a year you have seen people quit right before the breakthrough. This is one of the saddest things to me! People lack the grit and perseverance it takes to stick around and get the results. Our society is conditioned to want instant results. When those results don't happen right away, some people quit. Work on your perseverance and grit.

One of the very first people that signed up with me in network marketing told me that he didn't care how many new contacts he needed to make, he was going to sign up one hundred people before he gave himself the option to quit the business. This is a guy that had the right mindset! It wasn't about talking to one hundred people or only talking to friends and family. He was willing to sign up one hundred people before he even gave himself the option to quit. That is what perseverance and grit look like. This guy was willing to fail over and over again until he got to his goals.

You are going to have to give up some of your likes for some of your loves. You can't gain something new without giving up something old. Discipline can be a bad word or a scary word. I know that giving up something is scary, but it is a concept we need to understand.

The most vital thing that you have on this earth is your time. I love how one of my friends decided how to use her time every day. She told me that she imagines that every single hour of the day is worth a gold coin. Every day she wakes up with twenty-four gold coins that she has to use within the day. She asks herself, "How am I going to spend my twenty-four coins today?" Automatically, most of us use six to eight of those coins for sleep. But what are you going to do with the rest of those coins? How many gold coins are you going to spend on Netflix today? I loved thinking about time this way because it really is the most sought-after commodity in the history of the human race. It is even more precious than gold coins.

So, when I talk about giving up some of your likes for some of your loves, what I want you to do is, do it right now, or you can do it later. Take a piece of paper and divide it in half. On the left make a list of all your likes. On the right list all your loves. You may like watching several episodes on Netflix. Maybe sporting events. Golfing, shopping, getting drinks with friends, surfing social media—the list can go on forever. Now ask yourself, "What do I love?" You could love time freedom, serving, or money freedom.

I had to give up some of my likes. When I went to the gym, I chose to give up listening to music so I could grow in my leadership. I started using that time in the gym to listen to personal development. I had to give up my like of music for my love of leadership.

I'm not saying that you have to give up listening to music. Maybe that stays on your list. Everyone has outlets that help them stay balanced in life. Mine was watching movies with my wife. I would never give that up. But, once I understood the concept of giving up some of my likes for my loves I realized how much easier it is to obtain the things that matter most. It is incredible to be able to create that type of life for myself and my family.

When you are a failing learner you are always looking for opportunities for growth. Most often those experiences, opportunities, and resources aren't going to fall into your lap. You must be out there actively seeking knowledge and experience. So, ask yourself right now, "What am I willing to give up to actively seek more learning?"

## What you can do right now to work on being a failing learner:

- Write down the failures you have had in your business or personal life.

- Also write down the feedback you gained from the failure.

- Make your mess your message. Start to make the connection between failure, feedback, and grit to persevere.

- Be ok with failure from others. If you see yourself getting too carried away in others' failures, ask yourself why.

- Set goals that you are willing to go after regardless of the obstacles that come up for you.

- Face your fear of failure. How to you define failure? What are you worried will happen if you fail in public? - Fail big every quarter, small every single day, and EPIC once a year.

- Create a FAIL forward goal or goals. For example, you could create a goal of getting 100 people to say no to your business. Of course, your ultimate goal is a yes, but this exercise helps you overcome your fears. It helps you marry the process and date the results.

*"The true sign of intelligence is not knowledge but imagination."*

*– Albert Einstein*

# CHAPTER 3

# THE CREATIVE LEARNER

Tim Tebow is a famous American football and baseball star. Tim suffers from dyslexia, and so he couldn't learn to run the plays like other guys on his team. When Tim was younger, he struggled to learn the football routes like the other kids. It never made sense to him, and he started to get frustrated with the sport. Because Tim's father also suffers from dyslexia, he saw what was going on for Tim and knew he would need to help his son get creative as he learned how to look at the playbooks. "It has to do with finding out how you learn, and you really get it done quickly," Tebow said. "I'm not somebody that opens a playbook and just turns and reads and reads. That doesn't do it for me." Instead, Tim learned that making flashcards and memorizing them over and over again helped him learn the routes and plays.

Tim said, "You can be extremely bright and still have dyslexia. You just have to understand how you learn and how you process information. When you know that, you can overcome a lot of obstacles that come with dyslexia. When you figure out how you learn, you can accomplish whatever you want."

Maybe you are on the sidelines of your life because of a limiting belief about yourself. I have heard so many limiting beliefs in my career as a coach in network marketing. "I never finished high school." "Who am I to tell other people what to do?" "No one is going to want to work with a single mom who is struggling." "I have ADD, ADHD, dyslexia, etc."

You are in charge of your experience, and you have got to get creative about your learning. The more creative you can become, the better you will be at leading. Leading is about seeing differences in others and yourself and being willing and able to adjust and adapt your leadership based on what they need—not based on what you know how to do.

Learning looks different for all of us. In *The Game of Conquering*, I shared how I personally struggled with learning in school. One of the best things my mom did for me is not to allow that struggle to hold me back. She would talk with me about it, and then support me.

Instead of seeing your differences or others' as a weakness, you have got to see them as strengths that you can work with. People use things against themselves all the time. "I am shy." "I don't know how." "It is hard for me. It isn't my personality or nature." These are excuses that are holding you back from taking full ownership of your learning. You are the only one who suffers from your excuses.

Start to identify if learning a certain way isn't working for you. Then ask yourself, "What am I going to do to make sure I get the experience I need?" I have someone that has come to my masterminds in the past that gets distracted easily if she can see other people in front of her. She always asks to sit right in front so that she can stay focused. She also asked if I could make handouts or copies of the slides so she can follow along. I loved that she asked! She took control of her own learning and set herself up for the best success at the mastermind.

This also helps as you become a leader of others. When you can see that we all learn differently, and you start to get more creative with the learning process you can help accommodate more people on your team.

One of my clients always does her training with closed captioning on the bottom and the screen. She also includes a couple of small graphics to help the people that are more visual learners on her team.

If you have ever told yourself you are not good at learning, I am going to challenge you to stop saying that! You are a creative learner who is figuring out the best way you learn.

I have always tied my goals into my purpose. It helps to have a vision of where you are going. My goals have helped me tie into my deeper meaning and purpose. Have you ever seen someone make a goal that doesn't have a vision behind it? "I want to lose thirty pounds!" They proclaim. But why? What is the vision behind the goal? Do you want to hike a mountain, fit in a certain outfit for a special occasion? What is the reason behind the goal?

## Family Goals

When I was first married, my wife and I set a huge goal. We decided that when our kids turned twelve years old, we wanted to be able to take that child anywhere on a domestic trip and it would be with the opposite gender parent. We have two boys and two girls, so this worked out perfectly for us. I always say that I want to die with memories, not with dreams. We had the goal to spoil our kids with memories, not with material things they wanted. Once we made the goal, we got specific. I got the details of what this would look like.

We also decided at this same time that at age sixteen that child would get to go on a trip anywhere they want in the world. Yes, you read that right! I said, anywhere they want in the world, and they go with the same gender parent. It's been fun to be able to do several of these at twelve for two of my kids already now and we already have my daughter who's eleven who can't stop talking about what she wants to do when she's twelve.

In 2020 my son and I were able to go on his sixteen-year-old trip. At first, he couldn't decide where to go. He kept telling me he didn't have anywhere special he wanted to go. Then out of the blue, he came and told me he had made up his mind. He chose to go to Dubai. Six weeks later we headed to Dubai.

As a special surprise for my son, I treated him to everything first class. It was such an awesome experience to see my son's face light up seeing our seats in the first-class cabin on the flight. It got even better seeing him be able to take a drive in a Lamborghini, Ferrari and Porsche. We went skydiving, swam with sharks, went on a desert tour with my good buddy Frazer Brookes, and so many more experiences. It was such a crazy new experience for both of us.

The trip was epic. But the thing that hit me so hard while hanging out by the pool being able to talk with my son was that I was fulfilling one of my lifelong goals. I was in Dubai, sitting poolside with my sixteen-year-old son having those in-depth conversations. Huge goal accomplished that I can't wait to do with my youngest son when he is sixteen and I know my wife can't wait to take our girls. Ever since this one experience with my sixteen-year-old son, our relationship has improved dramatically. Those two weeks will always be remembered.

## Turn Vision into Reality

Vision leads to goals, which leads to actionable steps you can take to turn goals into reality. It all starts with visions. What do you want your life to look like? What experience do you want to create?

My vision is that I die with memories, not things. Over a decade ago, my wife and I created an epic goal for when we'll be grandparents (and you have to understand over a decade ago, I was still in my late twenties). At the time we made this goal, our kids were very young.

We created the goal that someday we want to be able to take all our kids, their spouses, and our grandkids on a trip, every single year. All expenses paid.

Let's put this into perspective. I have four kids. Let's say, they all get married. That means my wife and I are now paying for ourselves and eight other adults. If they all have two kids, you can see the math on that is pretty tremendous. Now we're at sixteen people! That is sixteen flights, accommodations, food, activities, and everything in between. That will add up quickly but again—die with memories, not with dreams.

These are big, huge goals that I've had, and they align perfectly with my vision. As you learn to lead, you must learn the role that vision has in your life and other people's lives as well. You must be willing to go all in with your own vision, so that you can show others the way. Your vision can start small. You can have a vision of paying cash for date night every single week. Awesome! Learn the value of the vision.

I had a huge goal that ties into my vision that I shared earlier. I made the goal thirteen years ago that I wanted to donate more money to charitable causes than what I was making at the time. In 2020, I was able to do that. I donated more money than what I was making thirteen years ago. Being able to donate that amount of money to charity and see how it has impacted other people's lives is a memory that I will never forget.

These are big goals that I have shared with you. Like I mentioned before, the vision helps set the goals. Your goals must be tied to vision. They must have a deep meaning to you. They must be specific. Specific goals drive!

I have many more goals, some big, some small. They all tie back into my vision. They all help me stay motivated and driven. Your goals have to be stronger than your objections. Your vision needs to be stronger than your mood swings. You will not make it in this business and be a leader of leaders unless you work on your vision. Good leaders have vision. Great leaders learn how to give vision. In the upcoming phases, I am going to teach you how to give vision, but it all starts with the vision you create for yourself.

The more effective you can be as a learner, the more you can become an effective leader. Once you master the skill of identifying your own weaknesses, utilize your resources, and ask for help you will be able to learn what you need to and then help others do the same.

I am not usually the person that comes in typically the fastest or the best. I'm someone that is tough, and I am persistent. I will stick around long enough to make things happen.

When I got started in network marketing, one of the very first things I did was start to observe and learn from the leaders that were already where I wanted to be. I looked at the incredible leaders who had huge success and I watched them intently.

I started to learn from each one by watching everything they did. I watched one leader every time he got on stage. He had a way of entering that got everyone pumped. It was fascinating to watch and start to learn from him how to do something as simple as walk on a stage. I had a bigger vision for myself. I knew that I wanted to be on stage one day, but I knew I lacked the skills. I didn't let that stop me from having my vision!

I learned several different aspects of network marketing and business by watching leaders that I admired. I knew I could learn anything, but I needed to be effective in my learning strategies. In other words, I had to learn how to learn.

The first strategy was to always extract the principle from everything I was learning. This one paragraph is one of the most important lessons of this book. Too many people confuse principles and techniques.

For example, my mentor used the following invite to approach prospects about network marketing. "Give me your credit card. We are going to make a ton of money together." This would be the stupidest invite ever for my style and personality. This is where so many network marketers get stuck and way too many get caught up in exact duplication. The technique is the words my mentor used. The principle is much different.

The principle I observed was the following. The world loves boldness. It makes people curious, and it is very contagious. The principle is to have a ton of energy in your approach and be excited about what you have. The technique varies.

For one they may be much louder and for another they will use completely different words. Whenever you are observing successful leaders observe and discover the principle. Your ability to learn how to learn will go to an entirely new level when you begin to focus on the principle and how to apply it with your own unique style and personality.

Another one of the strategies I used was watching, observing, taking notes, and then going and trying it myself. I would also watch the person and then imagine myself doing the same thing. I watched that leader walk on stage and pump everyone up, and then I would imagine what they would look, feel, and even smell like when I was the one doing it.

I began to create the future self that I needed to be able to draw upon, especially during hard times, during the times when I felt nervous, and the times when I felt uncomfortable. I want to remind you that no one gets a free pass from these feelings.

We all have a time of self-doubt, overwhelm, and nervousness. These are part of the game of learning and growing. If you can learn that now, you are WAY ahead of the curve. Most people aren't willing to struggle in order to grow. Struggling is the only way to success but if you learn and implement more effectively you will struggle for much less time.

## Shapeshifting

The best advice I can give people in this phase is—don't be a shapeshifter.

Think about the movies that have shapeshifters in them. A shapeshifter can become any person or object they want to be. They usually end up shifting into whatever thing is going to make it the least uncomfortable in that moment. If they need something, they shift. Shapeshifters spend their entire lives shifting themselves to get what they want.

There is a huge difference between progressing and shapeshifting. I am definitely not the same person I was three, ten, or twenty years ago. You want to be progressing and becoming a different version of yourself always, but the key is to stay true to yourself. Don't become a shapeshifter that becomes unrecognizable to your own self. Don't become something entirely different for the wrong reasons.

Shapeshifters are essentially people pleasers. They want everyone to like them, and so they go around shifting into what they think people want. I am a recovering people pleaser. I think most people can relate to wanting to impress or please others in order to fit in, feel good, and be part of the "in" crowd.

In my network marketing business, I tried to be the person that was available for everybody. If they messaged, texted, or emailed me, etc., I would be there for all of it. I wasn't being available to the people who deserved my time. I was spreading myself thin and I thought that made me a helpful and super supportive up-line leader. It wasn't. Instead, it was a huge stall in my progression. I was being ineffective and wasting my time trying to be everything to everyone.

In the end, I was filling my own ego and not being the leader to the people that most deserved my time. I was creating less of an income and less of an impact because I was spending my time with the time suckers. I wasn't creating an impact. In case you missed the above part, let me repeat it in different words. By people-pleasing, you think you are humble and servant-oriented but in reality, you are only serving your own unhealthy ego.

There is a great quote by an unknown author: "When you are twenty you care what everyone thinks. When you are forty you stop caring about what everyone thinks. When you are sixty you realize that no one was ever thinking about you in the first place."

This is really true, and I want to tell you that there is power if we can get to the place of the sixty-year-old mindset today. Stop worrying about if other people are thinking about you and realize that you are the only person thinking about yourself. Learn how to live with yourself, love yourself, and be your best advocate in the journey. No shapeshifting needed!

## The Honeymoon Stage

Marriage was much harder than I thought it would be. Being a dad is much harder than I thought it would be. My network marketing business was much harder than I thought it was going to be. So, we go through this honeymoon stage, while at some point you are going to get rejected by a friend or family member. You will have people judge you and say, "I can't believe you are doing that network marketing thing." You will have something that will affect your mindset. You are going through the process of recruiting yourself. It is key. The most important person you recruit is yourself. The only person that matters that you recruit is yourself. The only person you truly have to recruit is yourself. Once you have done that you will not only be able to grow an incredible team, but you will be able to attract an incredible team.

As you have this vision, understand this natural part of the process. I always heard that you get paid in direct correlation to your skill set and leadership. Although I think this is true, I think there is a missing aspect to this. This is the quote that I came up with which I already mentioned but needs to be mentioned again. Compensation always catches up to skill set and effort, but it is almost always massively delayed. I want you to reread that part. It is key that you understand that. When I started and was going through tough times my mentor told me this: "Network marketing can be the most underpaid business in the beginning. But it can become the most overpaid business in the end."

On the days that I was struggling the most or during my down times in the beginning, I would remind myself about what my mentor said. In my first December, I was not working effectively. I was working 80 hours a week in management mode and not doing that much. But I thought I was working very hard. I was so busy even though I wasn't being productive. I ended up having a paycheck for $372 that month. I thought I could work in fast food and make more than I just did. I was reminded about what my mentor told me, and I had to decide right then if I was willing to continue to work and figure it out, even if the paycheck was $372 a month. It can be the most underpaid in the beginning and the most overpaid in the end.

## The Sophomore Slump

Eventually, we move through that honeymoon phase and into the sophomore slump. This is where a lot of people get stuck. If you haven't been working on mindset and self-improvement, this is where you will get stuck. People in the sophomore slump aren't willing to quit the business, but they also aren't willing to look at themselves and invest in their mindset. They aren't willing to do the hard inner work that it takes to have that success.

And so, they are confused and think that production means being busy. They start to manage the team and think because they are busy, they are committed to having success. They are avoiding the top income-producing activities. They are working through this maintenance mode in their mind when in reality—maintenance mode doesn't exist. Let me say this again . . . Maintenance mode DOES NOT EXIST. You are either growing or you are slipping. Maintaining is fatiguing. Building is energy.

Be committed to your own personal development. Be the person that gets to be overpaid in this industry because you committed to your own development early on and stuck with the program. I have created one of the best planners that is specific for network marketing. It helps eliminate distractions, conquer big goals, and smash your to-do list. You can utilize it to schedule dedicated time to personal development, and income-producing activities. Don't get stuck in the sophomore slump!

## Boldness

Like I just mentioned, I learned by observing the principle from my mentor that the world loves boldness. When I did self-accountability, I knew I was lacking boldness as a quality. I also lacked the courage to try boldness on and figure out what my version looked like.

I had examples of boldness all around me with my successful mentors; I decided it was time to get uncomfortable and find my own version of boldness. I extracted that concept and principle from them and saw myself as the bold version of me.

Now the bold version of me was nowhere near the bold version of several of these leaders as they had different styles and personalities, but you can see how I took that concept and borrowed from the principal and applied it to my own style and personality. This helped me to be able to create the future self that I needed to become.

An effective learner is always figuring out how their own learning can translate into sales, training, and growth. Principle vs. Technique is key to your growth. An effective learner finds the principle and learns how to duplicate a technique that works for them.

## What you can do right now to work on being a creative learner:

- Check out the 90-day planner "The Network Marketing Strategy Planner/Tracker www.nwmstrategy.com.

- Learn how you learn best. Once you do, do everything you can to make sure you set yourself up to learn the best you can.

- Create your own learning plan and adjust to your own needs.

- Tie what you are learning to your goals and vision.

- Create a system of learning so that you are always working on self-improvement.

- Make a list of the resources you have available right now to learn them.

- Look at your time and dedicate a certain amount of time each week to learning.

- See who you have in your network that you can learn from. Use their time and yours wisely.

- This is the perfect time to set up a schedule for yourself. Stay accountable to the schedule.

- Learn how to stay on task and stick to what you say you are going to do.

I asked some of the top leaders in the network marketing industry what their tips would be for people in each phase. I thought it would be fun to share them with you to have some more perspective on what they see will help you really go all in and accomplish what you need to in this phase.

*"If your actions inspire others to dream more, learn more, or do, and become more; you are a leader."*

*– John Quincy Adams*

# CHAPTER 4

# THE SELF APPLIER

Milton Hershey, the founder of The Hershey Company, was a businessman and American chocolatier. He came up with the famous formula for the Hershey chocolate line, but it didn't happen overnight. Before creating America's favorite chocolate, Milton worked at several other candy factories. He was obsessed with the process of making all candy but found caramel and chocolate particularly fascinating. After countless hours perfecting his own recipes, he decided he would go out on his own to launch his own brand. It was a huge disaster. Twice he failed at starting his own business.

Milton was a self-applier, which means he was driven by self-motivation and always trying something new. He wasn't going to let failure stand in the way of his dream to become a household candy. He continued to apply himself. He traveled to Denver, New Orleans, and Chicago while learning from the best confectioners about their processes for making candy and chocolate. When he later returned home to his farm, he spent months perfecting the formulas. He was so passionate about his candy that he borrowed money from the bank to start a caramel company that finally became a huge hit. He based his new formula on his years of perfecting the candy and watching others make something similar.

He called his new company the Lancaster Caramel Company and it was a worldwide success. But Milton wasn't happy with just being a caramel company. He was still fixated on his chocolate recipe and creating a chocolate never before known by the world. In an unprecedented move, Milton sold the Lancaster Caramel Company for one million dollars and started the Hershey Chocolate Company.

Time and again, Milton had to apply what he was learning. He didn't settle for learning alone and working for someone else. He was driven by his vision and passion for working for himself and creating something the world had never experienced.

I often think about how much Mr. Hershey applied what he learned quickly. He was willing to face failures. He learned and then got straight into action. He was constantly observing, asking questions, and then going back into his business and applying what he had just learned. This is called the application phase of leadership. In the application phase, we focus on the feedback that we got in the learner phase. We focus on applying the feedback quickly and observing how it helps or gives us feedback for the next phase of business.

# STRONG FOUNDATION FIRST

Leaders in this phase are becoming leaders with several followers. But I want to remind you that leadership is built on a solid foundation. You don't "graduate" from different phases of leadership. In this phase of leadership, you are building on the solid foundation of leading yourself. You are not only doing the work for yourself, but people are watching what you are doing. The other important factor that I see leaders in this phase do is that they aren't waiting around for someone else to lead them or give them feedback. As a leader in the application phase, you apply yourself, and you don't wait around for someone else to tell you what to do. You don't sit in the "sophomore slump" telling everyone you need to learn one more thing. The applier knows when to learn and when to get up and get into action.

The Hershey chocolate bar wasn't made overnight. It took years for The Hershey Company to perfect their number one product. But those years weren't spent in "learner mode." They were learning, applying, evaluating, learning, applying, evaluating! Do you see the cycle?

For anyone to get the most out of their learning experience, you must use the cycle. Learn, apply, and evaluate. As a leader in the application phase, you will become a master of this cycle. Cycles are foundational work. Cycles help you to track what you are doing and see how you are progressing. When you can stick to a cycle, you have something to track.

Let's think about this in terms of network marketing skills. By now, you know how to contact people on your list. You know how to message people in messenger, but what happens if you never apply it? Then the education stops. There is nothing more to learn if you can't master the skill. I saw this all the time as a tennis coach. I would teach the tennis students a skill, but because they hadn't done anything with it, progress stopped. There is absolutely nothing to evaluate because you haven't performed! As a leader of followers, you will also be demonstrating by example the cycle you would like your newest team members or customers to start doing for themselves. Duplication is key here, and I promise you that people are watching you. If you "take a break" from your keystone habits, that will be seen and felt by others, and they will mirror that.

One of my mentors gave me some great advice that goes along perfectly with becoming a self-applier. He said, "If you strip away all the fluff in network marketing, the best thing you can do to become a leader is first to empower yourself to make the right choice, and then go and empower others." Empowering yourself can feel extremely uncomfortable, especially when you haven't yet had that success. But you have to empower yourself on what you're committed to.

When we first start network marketing, we have uplines and leaders that believe in us probably more than we believe in ourselves. But if we are going to get anywhere in network marketing, we need to work on becoming our own biggest advocate. We have to learn to believe in ourselves more than anyone else. Sure, we will have down times and doubts that creep in. That is when support from uplines, leaders, and coaches can be beneficial, but no one can be your sole belief source.

# SELF-BELIEF

As a leader in this applier phase, you will be working intensely on your self-belief. Being a self-applier means that you aren't waiting, wishing, or wanting anyone else to show up for you better than you show up for yourself. A self-applying leader also works on their belief about their future and being able to create the future they want to have. One of the exercises I take my personal clients through is called "borrowing from the future." You can do this exercise right now.

Think about that future version of yourself. How does that future version of yourself show up? What type of belief does the future version of you have about you and your business? If you can't see your future version OR if you have a negative perception of the future you, it is time to get some coaching on your beliefs. As a self-applier, it is important that you see the future version of yourself as a higher version of your present self. The self-applying leader works on their future.

I said that you need to empower yourself before you can empower others. That is a fact. Your newest team members are going to need you to communicate and believe in them. Remember, as a leader of a follower, you have one or more people that are looking to you. That is difficult to do when you lack self-belief.

I tell my kids this all the time, "Even if you don't know it, you have people that are watching you. They are looking to you to see what type of example you are going to set." This is 100 percent true in this phase of leadership. Leaders in the application phase tell me, "But no one is watching me." That isn't true. You just don't know that they are watching you. But your followers are watching, your family, your friends, your leaders, and mentors. You have eyes on you right now, and they are watching to see how you show up.

Stephen Covey says his definition of leadership is communicating to others ones worth and potential so well that they see it in themselves. So, your goal is, first and foremost, to create a vision for yourself. Your goal is to be able to help empower yourself to see yourself better than you ever have before. Once you have done that, go out and do it for others.

Think about it. If you have become a self-applying leader, that means that all of the work you are asking others to do, you have done yourself. You can start to see where their roadblocks may be because you have done it, too. You can start to see and feel what self-belief looks like because you are starting to have it yourself!

When the newest person comes in, you get where they are coming from. You know they may struggle with self-belief or doubt. You know they may not even think it is possible to make millions of dollars in this industry. When you help them create their own vision, you can talk with them about maybe having a bit of extra spending money or being able to make an extra payment on their car. YOU are now that leader that is giving vision to others and meeting them where they are at.

I can always tell when people haven't worked on their own self-belief. One of the major signs is when they aren't able to meet people where they are at starting in network marketing. I see people paint these elaborate made-up visions and promise too much. This is a huge sign that they don't believe in themselves because they haven't gone through the process of self-belief. They think it is all imaginary, so their imagination creates some completely fictional story to "sell."

Don't be that person. Start applying and working on your own self-belief. Start small and work your way into a bigger vision. This helps you through the process that your newest person will be working through. It creates an authentic vision that can then be built upon, and you create a bond and trust with your team.

Going through this process is what all good leaders do. First, apply the principles yourself, and then go and help others do the same. Empower yourself, and then empower others. Start with a vision and a self-belief, and then stretch yourself to see what the future version of you is capable of. Become a leader, and then a better leader.

## What you can do right now to work on being a self-applier:

- Journal these questions: "What do I believe about myself right now?" "What do I want to believe about my future self?" "In what areas of my life does belief feel hard?" "What belief am I willing to work on until I am successful?"

- Write down a list of empowering thoughts and keep them somewhere you can see them daily.

- Intentionally look at those thoughts and say them out loud to yourself.

- Ask people that you trust and look up to what they believe about you. Borrow that belief if you have to and work on believing it for yourself.

- Stay committed to your keystone habits.

- Now create your own personal story in an empowering way. What are your accomplishments? Dig deep because I often hear many say they don't have any when in reality they do.

*"The strength of the team is each individual member. The strength of each member is the team."*

*— Phil Jackson*

# CHAPTER 5

# THE TEAM
# APPLIER

Google has spent the past ten years perfecting teamwork. In fact, they were so committed to figuring out what made a great team that they spent millions of dollars researching teamwork and had a special project named "Project Aristotle" that was all put together for the research of teamwork.

After Google's exhaustive efforts they came to some interesting conclusions about what makes up a great team. Their findings revealed that the best team members show sensitivity and listen to one another. They also see the importance of sharing their story and encouraging their team to do so too.

At the conclusion of Google's research, they described psychological safety as the most important factor in building a successful team. They also found that the best teams invite team members to contribute to the conversation and respect one another's emotions. It has less to do with who is in a team, and more with how the members interact with one another. Think about how you are interacting with your team as their leader. Do you ask for a contribution? Do you apply the listening skills or learn some if you are lacking them?

Great leaders boost their ability to listen and to be sensitive to their team members. As a leader in network marketing, it will be your job to think about how you create safety, sensitivity, and a culture of listening to everyone on the team. This isn't something that just happens!

As we talk about being a team applier, this is going to mean something different for everyone. You may find that you are great at showing empathy and listening to others, but you lack the skill of teaching and getting the team excited for promotions. You may be a great motivator but lack the skills to listen. We talked in the previous phase about knowing your own strengths and weaknesses. In this phase, we are building on that. In the applier phase, I want you to know what your weaknesses are and be able to see how they are impacting your team.

One of my clients told me she got uncomfortable every time someone shared a vulnerable story. She wasn't used to sharing emotions openly and so when others did, she would ignore it. This made her look like an unsympathetic leader, but really, she was a leader who hadn't learned how to open up like the people on her team. She was a leader who didn't know how to apply sensitivity.

This is why building on the leadership phases is so important. As soon as she identified that she lacked the skill of sensitivity, we were able to create a learning plan around it. She started with phase one and learned through the leadership process how to have more sensitivity and empathy towards other people. Then one day she was meeting with a woman, and she said, "It clicked! All my empathy training set in and as this woman shared her struggles with me, I wasn't uncomfortable and wanting to move her away from sharing. I leaned into it and listened."

She took what she had learned in the learning phase of leadership and applied it with one of her team leaders. She was being an example of what the phases of leadership look like in network marketing! So, think back to phase one. What are the areas that you committed to learning more about? How has that been going, and what are you willing to start to apply?

Each team and leader is different. As we talk about these concepts, you have to be able to find the balance for yourself and what feels right. This book is an opportunity for you to gauge your skills as a leader and then decide what you want to strengthen and work on.

# HARD CONVERSATIONS

I have the opportunity to coach several clients one on one throughout the year. Time and time again I have been coaching on the same topic. I just had this conversation come up three times this morning with high-level six-figure earners. They all asked about how to have tough conversations with a team member. An interesting thing about all of them - they know the conversation needs to happen, but they are feeling really resistant to having it. Part of becoming a leader is being willing and able to have ANY conversation that needs to take place. Maybe this is you. Maybe you are willing to cheer people on, but if you have to hold them accountable or correct them, you cower away. This is a perfect opportunity for you to show up as an applying leader.

One of the skills that you are learning at this phase of leadership is communication. You have got to start communicating with your customers and new team members. Think about your own leader and what you liked about how they showed up for you. Think about how you wish hard conversations would have gone, and then apply that knowledge to the conversation you need to have.

People get stuck between the learning and applying phases of leadership because they aren't willing to have any conversation with their team members. I was talking with this one individual who is making six figures a month in her business. She doesn't want to work with someone on her team because this person's extremely negative. As we were coaching, this leader told me that she didn't want to offend her team member. What is more offensive? The fact that the leader isn't willing to give feedback OR the fact that she is ignoring having the conversation? When you hold back from giving feedback to others because of how they may react negatively to you, you are being selfish.

This goes right back to having crucial conversations with your team members. So let me give you a six-step process to having difficult or crucial conversations with people on your team.

1 - Identify the problem. Why is it a problem for you? Why is it a problem for them? Is there anyone else that it is a problem for and why?

2 - Do your own work first! This means that you have to be willing to get over frustration, anger, fear, etc., in order to have the conversation from a neutral place. Write it all down, talk to your upline or mentor about it.

3 - Come from love. Seriously, this one is the biggest one. If you can't have the conversation from love, go back to step #2. You need to love and care about the person in order to have the conversation.

4 - Ask open-ended questions throughout the conversation. An open-ended question is a question that gets people to give more than a "yes/no" answer. Instead of asking "Is this a problem?" you could ask, "What do you think is the problem?" Very different answers! See where they are at and what their thinking is about what is happening.

5 - Don't take it personally. People say things as they are processing through and having conversations. If someone says something that hurts you, don't take it personally. You will see that oftentimes in the heat of the moment people say things without thinking about what they are saying. In these conversations especially.

6 - Come with one solution in mind and be open to hearing their solutions. I never want to talk just to talk. You should be having these conversations with some solutions in mind. Be willing to hear their solutions and then work from there.

These steps have helped so many people learn to have those hard conversations. As a leader, you must learn to communicate through all situations. Team applying leaders are not selfish. They are willing to take their knowledge about feedback and use it in their own team. They are willing to give feedback swiftly from a place that feels empowering. They are also willing to have tough conversations from a future self-perspective. Meaning that they see that their future self will thank them for having the conversation now, instead of putting it off and thinking that it will go away. Remember, rich people think long term whereas poor people only think short term. This applies to all aspects of your life—financially, spiritually, mentally, and physically.

I talked about this type of conversation in *The Game of Networking*. You can be very direct and even what people call harsh, as long as you convey your intent. What is the intent behind the feedback and conversation you are having? If you can convey the intention first before you have the conversation, it helps others know where you are coming from before having the conversation and giving feedback. Think back to when my mentor told me I was a terrible presenter. I was great with the feedback because I knew the intent that was behind that feedback.

If you can communicate from a point of feedback, it allows the person to see that you care. I do want to point out that the person you are talking to may take it the wrong way, and that's ok. You have to allow them to have whatever reaction they are going to have. But you get to know that you came from the best intentions possible.

Leaders have swift to the point conversations with the best intent. They apply their leadership skills and don't avoid crucial conversations. I see so many "leaders" that have become the "avoiders." They start avoiding the tough conversations and the necessary conversations because they are uncomfortable. They don't work on their intent, and they stay annoyed and silent with their team members.

# CARE ENOUGH TO SAY IT

I have another woman who I am working with, and she knows that one of her team members needs to sponsor more customers. The way their company has set up their payment structure, an individual can make the most amount of bonus if they have a certain number of customers under a couple of builders. This particular team member always goes after business builders and shies away from getting customers on her team. Her leader can see that if she continues this pattern in her business, she is going to miss out on some huge bonuses. She has to get more customers, and her leader knows it.

The leader told me, "I don't know what to do. I may just work around her and add my own customers. I don't know what she would think if I told her to focus on customers." This leader would rather work around her team members than have a crucial conversation and tell her leader how to optimize the compensation plan. This is crazy! As a leader, we must apply the knowledge and expertise that we have to help our own team grow.

You have got to care enough to say it. My wife once saw a lady leaving the bathroom with her dress tucked into her pantyhose. My wife ran up and stopped the woman from leaving and told her what she saw. The woman was embarrassed initially but so grateful that my wife was willing to tell her. Don't let your team members walk around having their business being "exposed." You have got to care enough to say it to them. There is a good chance that her team member has no idea that she is creating a gap. You have got to get over your own uncomfortableness in order to help others grow. This phase doesn't mean you are an expert, but you are also further along than your followers. As a team applier, you are learning, applying, and evaluating.

As you evaluate, you are going to be getting feedback from yourself or your leader. This is a great time to share that feedback with the person on your team that needs to hear it. Don't let them make the same mistakes as you because you are withholding feedback or not comfortable having conversations.

I always say, whatever you do well as a leader will only duplicate sometimes, but whatever you do poorly will almost always duplicate. Often, I have companies that come and consult with me, and last year I had a company come to ask about communication training.

They were running up against a culture within the company of not having crucial conversations. Everyone was talking around the problem and not sitting with the right people talking about the right things. I met with the CEO and leadership team and guess what I found? The communication block was coming from up top! The leadership team themselves were finding it hard to communicate and have direct conversations. The entire company duplicated, and it became part of their culture. After coaching with me and showing them how to have direct conversations with intent, their company culture is turning around, and their leadership team and builders are all on board and now having direct conversations with intent. You must apply your intent and have those tough conversations.

A team applier is also willing to train before they are ready. Remember back to my experience of presenting in front of the team before I was ready and getting that feedback from my mentor? That wasn't comfortable for me. Right before I got on, I wondered why my mentor was letting me do this training because it felt like I wasn't qualified. But I gave it my best, because I wanted to do whatever he told me to do.

In the applying phase of leadership, you are going to be doing many things that you don't feel ready for. Being uncomfortable is the currency of your dreams, so get used to paying with it!

## What you can do right now to work on being a team applier:

- Find the team skill that you need to work on and be willing to start in the learning phase with it.

- Think about how you want to run a team and start applying those skills right now no matter how large the team is.

- Empathy, compassion, and asking for contribution are going to help you become a great team leader.

- Really work on your listening skills. What do you hear in what people are saying? What do you hear in what people are NOT saying?

- Be willing to have tough conversations.

- Say yes and volunteer before you are ready.

*"Great leaders are almost always great simplifiers, who can cut through argument, debate and doubt, to offer a solution everyone can understand."*

*— General Colin Powell*

# CHAPTER 6

# THE STRATEGIC APPLIER

In a study done in 2018, one hundred CEOs were polled about what they thought made them great leaders. Ninety percent of them mentioned "strategy" being a skill that they saw as making them great leaders. So how does applying strategy help you become a great leader? Strategy is always involved in a great business plan. I hear some people in network marketing talk about how they just love their team, and the rest works itself out. I hate to break it to you, but loving on your team is a strategy, and as much as I love love . . . it cannot be the only strategy in place when you are becoming a leader of a successful team. Love can be PART of your strategy, but if you ever check your numbers at the end of the month, you have another strategy at play too. As a strategic applier, leaders own up to all the strategies that they have. They don't feel bad about strategy, and they don't shy away from it. They see it as an integral part of their business.

To become a strategic leader, you must be willing to unapologetically apply several key components and strategies to your business. Let's talk about strategy. If you look strategy up in the dictionary, it says: "A plan of action or policy designed to achieve an overall aim." It is safe to say that we all have strategy in play most of the time in our life. You all probably know by now how much I love playing games. Games are a huge part of our family and friends. Every time we play a game, I am always thinking about what strategy plan is going to win the game for me. You should be doing the same thing in your business. Instead of seeing strategy as a bad word in business, let's first own that we all have strategy and that we are going to use it for the benefit of our business.

People shy away from strategy for a couple of reasons. First, they struggle to own that they are creating a business. These are my lovers. These are the people that say they just want to love on people. These are also the people that are afraid of other people's opinions. They have justified their business by masking it as a way to help. Guess what . . . It can be both. But you must accept and embrace that your BUSINESS in the WAY you help others.

Another reason people shy away from strategy is their belief that strategy is a hard complex thing that they know nothing about. This may be your first business, but that doesn't mean you can't learn. Think back about the learning chapters on leadership that we just covered. Strategies can be simple. You can learn strategies. Don't become your own obstacle by telling yourself you can't learn strategies.

Next, I want you to define what you want your business to look like. Who will you serve? How will you serve them? We talk more in depth about this in the coming chapters, but if you can answer those two questions, you have a strategy plan. Well done! Now let's apply your strategy plan to your business.

After you have defined your strategy plan of who you serve and how you help them, define your role as a leader. I like to say this is the "who do you want to be?" in leadership. There are all sorts of ways to lead. You can lead as a coach, a dictator, a best friend, or a motivator. Create the role you play as the leader to clearly see how it helps your strategy to lead. Some of the greatest leaders in military history have been gentle, soft-spoken men at home, but when they lead their armies, they take on a different role as a leader.

You are moving right along in creating strategy! Next, think about the strategy plan that includes systems and processes. Every single company has a system created on how to be successful. Maybe even your upline has created systems. Decide for yourself what systems you want to apply and how they will be part of your strategy. Don't reinvent the wheel here! You don't need to necessarily come up with your own systems. You need to apply and use the ones that work.

Strategy and vision are a leader's best allies when it comes to building. Vision keeps us motivated, and strategy helps us keep moving forward. You can't have one without the other, but too often in network marketing, people forget to lead with both. Visionary leaders get stuck dreaming and imagining. Their systems are haphazard at best and real progress is hard to make. Strategic only leaders get caught up in the system and make everyone follow it precisely. They become their own bottlenecks because of their lack of vision for the future.

As you learn to apply strategy, use these three steps to make sure you are keeping the vision in alignment with the strategies you are using. A great leader applies strategy to become the bridge between the ideas they have for the business, and the action that needs to happen to make it successful.

# DON'T COMPLICATE THE SYSTEM

I love having the chance to coach leaders that are brand new to network marketing and have a team of three to four people. But I also get fired up to coach leaders of leaders who are earning seven figures and have teams of hundreds of thousands of people. The other day I was coaching someone that was new to my seven-figure mastermind group. I asked her how it felt to be the first million-dollar earner in her company. She said, "Overwhelmed and stressed out! People keep asking me how I did it. Even the owner of the company wants me to teach people how I did it. I am feeling burnt out on being the HOW person for everyone."

This leader doesn't want to disappoint her team or company, and so she came to me to ask me to help her create an elaborate system to show people how to have success. I told her I couldn't help her. It's not that I didn't want to, but I have seen this all before and it is a big problem. She wanted to create a system that has never been done before to "show" people how to have success. She personally wasn't using this system when she built her business, so why would she think it was key to her success? I have seen other people create these elaborate systems, and they have essentially created a system that will kill their success.

They end up creating a system that is so good that it is bad for the business. The system uses all the latest and greatest tools, it is complex, and takes people a certification process to learn how to do it. It is NOT what the successful leader used to build but is now marketing it to their team and company as the latest and greatest way to build.

When this leader started out, she was using tried and true simple duplicatable steps to build. But now, she wanted to create an entirely new system that she had never used. This is teaching everyone to build their business with a fake system that hasn't created duplicatable success.

I want you to understand that the best systems are the simplest systems. I have mentioned this from the beginning of the book. Keep it simple! As a strategic applier, I don't want you to get trapped in a strategy that becomes too elaborate or confusing. A strategic applying leader keeps it simple. But how simple . . . you may be asking. At the beginning of the book, I shared how my income dropped drastically. It was because I got stuck creating complicated systems! I am so passionate about this because I was the guilty party doing this!

Systems should be so simple that a fifth grader could follow and understand them. Why a fifth grader? Because studies have shown that the average person's mental capacity is that of a fifth grader. Here is the best part, a simple system will duplicate time and again and you won't need to prequalify people to be on your team by asking people, "Do you have a master's degree?"

That's the power in a system. Don't get caught up in having a complex complicated system. It will kill your business. The companies and teams that have the most amount of momentum are always the ones with the simplest system. Growing a larger team is the exact time you want to look and see how to simplify your systems. Ironically, this is when teams create more complex systems. What works is what duplicates.

I'm giving you this based on experience. I've created some of the best systems that were so good, they were absolutely awful because they were way too complex. I loved my systems. They made sense to me, because of my experience and expertise in the business. Those systems failed hard because they weren't simple. I had to go back and simplify so that anyone could follow them. I had to challenge the system and make it simple. I would ask myself, "Is this something every single person could understand?" Another great question, "Is this something that even the person with the worst skill set in the world can do?"

We all know and love those people. It could be a friend, but their skill set on a scale of one to ten is a one or two. Can they execute and follow this system? Could they understand this system?

I am going to encourage you as you step into becoming a leader that is strategically applying what they have learned; do not become a leader that makes it complicated to follow into success. Create and follow systems that everyone can follow. I am going to challenge you to be a leader that simplifies your actions and makes them easy to apply. Make it simple to get the type of success you are having.

# A LITTLE MORE ACTION

To step into an applying leader, you must continue taking your own action in business and get other people to do the same thing. Get your team into action using the simple system. I love the lyrics to Elvis' song: "A little less conversation a little more action." My take on this is "A little less learning and talking and a little more action and application!" Do not become the broke, know it all!

We all know the people that are preparing to get ready for the conversation to ask if they are ready to talk about the business. If you know, you know!

Here is an easy way to think about it. You know the cycle by now! Learn, apply, evaluate.

Unfortunately, many systems are so challenging that they keep people in learning mode for way too long. Your system should be easy enough that someone can learn and apply it immediately. If the average person cannot take that action right away, you have got to simplify.

I was able to scale massively and crush new ranks because the system was simple. I was able to hit ranks and qualify for those incentive trips because I kept it simple and took massive action. I didn't have time to sit around and create complex systems to confuse and keep people learning. As a team, we learned a simple system and went and put it into action over and over again.

As a leader, I want you to apply this principle. Keep it simple. Have a little less conversation, and a little more action! Here is a crazy simple insight that you probably already know but may need a reminder for creating any system. Working in this business is talking to brand new people about your business or products. All systems should emphasize how to not only do this but also to spend 80 percent of your time here.

I talked briefly about using a calendar or scheduling system in the last phase. I want to mention it again here. Scheduling your time is crucial. Don't believe me? I want you to do an exercise for me. For the next two days write down what you do during the day. Preferably write it down as you change from one activity to the next. I do this on my phone. Write down what the activity was and how long it took you. You will be shocked to see where your time is going.

One woman did this, and she said she had no idea how much time it was taking her to go grocery shopping and put the groceries away. She said she usually "zones out" at the grocery store. She was shopping for one hour! That doesn't include driving home and putting the groceries away. Now, if you want to spend one hour at the grocery store, that's fine, but we are so often giving our time away to things that we don't want to be. Do this exercise and see where you are giving your time away. Next, set up a scheduling system that works for you. You can find my personal scheduling system at www.sperrybonus.com.

## What you can do right now to work on being a strategic applier:

- Start with your strategy plan. Who do you help? What do you offer? How do you want to be seen?

- Work on having conversations about everything. Use the six-step system to have hard conversations with team members.

- Write out your systems for onboarding, sales conversations, and any other DMO that you have. Ask yourself if they are duplicatable and are easy to use.

- Check back with your vision—does it align with the strategy? If not, get it in alignment!

- Keep it simple. Strategy is about execution and not the complexity of the steps. Continue to use your planner and see what action you are taking that is moving you forward.

*"To invent you need a good imagination and a pile of junk."*

*– Thomas Edison*

CHAPTER 7

# THE CREATIVE APPLIER

Madam C.J. Walker was the first woman to become a self-made millionaire in the United States of America. Walker's parents were slaves who later became free, and she was their first child to be freeborn.

Madam Walker had lived with a scalp ailment that resulted in hair loss, and she couldn't find any product that helped. Out of her own creativity, desire, and resilience, she invented a line of African American hair products. She found them helpful to so many people that she promoted her products by traveling around the country giving lecture demonstrations and eventually established Madame C.J. Walker Laboratories to manufacture cosmetics and train sales beauticians.

She said, "I got my start by giving myself a start." Madam C.J. Walker was such an amazing example of applying her creativity to create something that had never been done before.

Part of creativity is coming up with dreams and visions for your future. Every single great organization has a vision. Can you imagine Apple removing Steve Jobs' vision from the company? It wouldn't be the same company! That vision put the company on the map and lives on even though he is gone. It is important to understand the power of vision.

Vision is what motivates people. Nobody lacks motivation. They lack vision. The first thing you need to create is your own vision. Let me tell you what I mean by that, because often in our industry vision is a buzzword that so many people use, but not everyone knows what that means.

Vision is what you dream your future looks like. Vision can be about next week or twenty years from now. Vision is creating our future from our imagination. Vision is allowing ourselves to believe in something that is not yet real. When we start to create a vision, understand that it may not be some big grand thing. Your vision may be that next month you would like to make enough money to take your family out to dinner. That's great! Rarely does anyone start out having the biggest, clearest vision ever. Our vision grows with us. As we go through trials, sacrifices, and success your vision will grow.

I coached a woman who had a vision that she could take her family to Disneyland for a day. I asked her if she would be buying food and souvenirs while she was there. She looked at me like I was crazy. "You think I can afford that?! Slow down, Rob Sperry, I am working on envisioning me getting through the gates!" Her vision could only take her that far right then. I told her we would start with the front gates and go from there. It was the perfect place to start. We worked on stretching her vision and thinking about what it would take to not only get in the gates but eat at Disneyland too.

This same woman messaged me on Facebook a year later. She sent me a picture of her family in Disneyland eating at one of the restaurants. She said, "Ok, Rob Sperry, that vision and belief stuff got us through the front gates, riding every single ride, and spending some ridiculous amount of money on some chicken nuggets. If you can do that, I'm pretty sure you might be Peter Pan himself. Let's work on a new vision when I get home." Always be working on your own vision. Just because you can't see yourself there right now, doesn't mean you won't be able to do that in the future. As a creative applier, you are leading the front in vision and belief.

As I always say good leaders have vision; great leaders give vision. The next level is being able to convey vision to others. People will borrow your vision many times when they begin. Think back about the woman I was coaching. She had to borrow my vision of dining in Disneyland. She hadn't arrived yet at what was possible for her and her family. This is why your vision is so important. If you haven't worked on your own, then what will you let people borrow?

Look at all the incredible leaders that we've had throughout the course of history. When people are struggling, they would borrow vision. Vision is confidence. Vision tells us that we are willing to imagine a life where we have the experiences we have always wanted. People feel like they are being let down if their vision never comes to life, so they don't allow themselves to dream and set big goals. As a creative applying leader, it is now your job to see when people lack confidence and let them borrow your vision.

When people were struggling, they looked to Gandhi, Martin Luther King Jr., and other people who had a clear vision. Your vision could be where people look when they are struggling. Borrowing vision is how you start to become a leader. Think back to phase one of leadership. You were just learning how to create vision. You may have had to borrow your upline's vision for a bit while you worked on your own. Now, as a leader of followers, you are lending vision while other people create their own. You are showing people what you believe is possible in your own life, and then allowing them to do the same thing in theirs.

# YOU CREATE YOUR OWN POSSIBILITIES

As leaders, we are always working on our creativity. We want to be able to push what we see is possible. We want to be able to dream bigger than we have been allowed to and think up things no one else has. As adults, we are taught that creativity is something for children. Often, our creativity has been stifled by others. We are told that we always have to be right, and few things hinder creativity like perfection. Remember, this goes back to failure and not wanting to be seen as wrong. Sometimes creativity is seen this way.

We must be able to apply creativity and allow ourselves to fail. Malcolm Gladwell did a study that talked about how child geniuses don't have much success because they are praised so much for being smart that they stop creating enough ideas to make lots of failures and have one epic success. Their fear of failure stifles their creativity.

I want you to think about this as if you're creating a movie. And the person is watching your movie. They don't see themselves as being in the movie, but we can cast the vision about how they can create their own movie. And not only create a movie but be the starring role! We are telling them, "You are capable of doing this." Sharing our vision and inviting people to create their own vision is helping us consistently show people what is possible.

Most people don't lack motivation, they lack vision. When the vision is clear enough, people are willing to do whatever it takes to make that vision become a reality. Getting through the gates and eating in Disneyland did not just happen overnight for the woman I was coaching. It took her a solid year of perseverance, dedication, and work. She was willing to make sacrifices, overcome obstacles, and create small wins because her vision became so rock solid.

The next question I get asked constantly is, "How do you give vision?" I started talking about this briefly in chapter four, but I want to add to the topic here because it goes along well with becoming a creative applier in leadership. It's much easier to give vision when you have done the work of empowering yourself, believing in yourself, and mapping out your future. Giving vision is built on the foundation of empowerment, belief, and future self-work that you have done already. Like I mentioned in Chapter four, start by empowering, believing, and mapping out your future.

Next, I always like to give examples through stories. We know that people connect through story, and as a creative applier, you should always be able to share a story to help teach and lead.

Let's say someone is stuck feeling like this business is hard, and they will never make the type of money they want to. What type of vision is going to be best for me to create for them? I could give them statistics about traditional business, OR I can tell them a story and sprinkle the stats into the story. What do you think will go over better with your team members?

Tell a story or paint a vision for the person that is struggling. This skill is one that leaders who are creative appliers know very well. If this guy is feeling like a failure, he may not see the vision of the business. You could paint a picture for him to think about the amount of debt some professionals go into to get training. Think about how much debt a doctor is in once he/she graduates from medical school. They may not even have a job after having invested in all that training. How long do you think it will take for that doctor to pay off their student debt? By no means are we putting down a doctor or any profession. We are only giving perspective to the current situation.

You have to become the storyteller of your life. If you want to become a great leader, become a great storyteller. Record yourself telling your story of how you started in network marketing. Think about where you were before you started network marketing. Think about the problem that you were having and how network marketing helped you solve it. Tell the story of how you were the hero of your own life or the lives of your family. Once you record it, share it! Stories get lost when we stop telling them. Post it on social media with the #mynetworkstory. If you are ever feeling stuck or frustrated with your business, go and watch some of these stories. You will be inspired to go out and help others!

## BELIEVING FOR OTHERS BEFORE THEY CAN DO IT FOR THEMSELVES

When we talk about becoming a creative leader, we want to think about putting things into perspective for the team. You are creating vision by giving the people perspective and giving them different ways to see things. As a leader, you will need to work on casting vision for others.

We also talked about helping others believe in themselves. I can't stress enough how important self-belief is. Like I mentioned in Chapter four, work on your self-belief first and then help others. Could you imagine leading a team of people that had full belief in themselves? That is an unstoppable group of people!

Belief comes from our thoughts. A great place to work on other people's beliefs is to start to see what they think of themselves. You can do team or individual exercises where you have the team or person write down all their thoughts about themselves. This helps them to see how they speak to themselves. Do they have negative self-talk? Do they even think about themselves? Start by having people become aware of how they are talking to themselves, and it will give you great perspective on how much self-belief your team has. As I have mentioned before, this book is set up to be a self-study and application in leadership, but it is also set up to help you train your teams to be leaders.

One other strategy that changed everything for me was a simple question. Could the person you are sponsoring become better than you? Of course, they can. You can teach them the mistakes you made as well as the success lessons your team has taught. Stop making yourself the issue when you are casting a vision. The person you are sponsoring or have already sponsored has all the potential in the world. Don't allow your insecurities and weaknesses to hinder them.

If you find that people are struggling in your team with their self-belief, start them in phase one and walk them through the leadership phases.

This is all about creating. You need to be in creation mode to come up with vision, perspective, and help others work on their belief. You have to become a leader that can see the potential future that others could have if they are willing and want it. As you work on this, I want you to see for yourself if you have any negative self-blocks that are standing in your way of creating vision, perspective, and futures for other people or yourself.

## What you can do right now to work on being a creative applier:

- Check back in with your vision, goals, and belief. Have them set so that you can help others create their own. Remember, you are leading by example!

- Work on casting vision for other people. Show them the way to dream big and take action towards that dream.

- Have beliefs in others. Share those beliefs with them and impact their lives with your own belief.

- Create a story or vision board on your computer of stories that could help motivate others. Record your own story and share it as #mynetworkstory,

- Set up your schedule!

# TOP TEN TIPS FROM TOP LEADERS ABOUT THE LEARNER PHASE

1 - In the learner phase, communication is key to how to communicate with your leaders and the people you are selling to.

2 - Daily methods of operation are crucial! Duplicatable systems.

3 - Don't DIY your systems, duplicate from people that already have them and are successful.

4 - Build authentic relationships with team members and their clients. We are not selling a product. We are selling who we are.

5 - Part of your personal development should be learning how to manage your money. Learn how to manage money even before you have it! Your millionaire self will thank you!

6 - Learn how to build confidence in yourself, the company, the product, your upline, and your downline.

7 - Use an onboarding system and teach your newest leaders to do the same. Duplicate everything!

8 - Learn to be brave and to start conversations with people. Learn how to have a conversation that is a two-way process, not a "presentation." Learn to listen to their needs MOST of the time . . . not pitching your product or opportunity.

9 - Invest your time and money into yourself and your development. Make one of your keystone habits personal development for sure!

10 - Be the leader of one . . . YOURSELF. Start there and be 100% committed to being the best leader and follower for yourself. Others will join you soon!

## The Lifestyle Phase $10k–$100k

# THE 3 PHASES OF LEADERSHIP
## THE FOUR STAGES

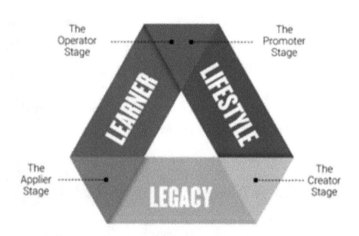

The lifestyle phase of network marketing is where people are past survival. In the lifestyle phase, people are making between $10k–$100k annually. They may be doing network marketing full time, and their paychecks from their business are now covering many, if not all, of their basic necessities. This is where people start focusing on their lifestyle. With their basic needs met people start to believe in themselves and what they can create. I often see people start to dream again in this phase!

In the lifestyle phase of the business, this group of people has proven that they know how to follow. They are taking care of their DMOs and are following the system set in place for themselves. They are also showing others how to do the same. In this phase, you are learning how to inspire others and be the inspiration your team needs to look up to. You will also learn how to outsource the things you don't need to do, and delegate responsibilities through the team. The best leaders learn how to delegate and learn what is most important for them to be doing.

In the introduction, I talked about how the lifestyle phase is where you will build on being a leader of followers. This is where you will start to master selling with stories and building your confidence around sharing. You will learn how to create and motivate contacts, take people through a system, and learn how to duplicate that system over and over again. As you do this, you will move into being a leader of another leader. You will have made such an impact that someone will want to be doing what you are doing, and you will learn to show them how.

The lifestyle phase is also where you learn to become even more coachable. You will learn how to use feedback and personalize it. This means taking accountability that your business is YOUR business. Every success and failure are yours. When you get feedback, learn something new, or get data showing you something about your team; it is your job to decide what to do with it.

I see this phase of people hitting roadblocks in two different areas. First, compare and despair. As you watch other people in this phase living out their dreams, you start to compare yourself, your business, and your own lifestyle choices. This can be a dangerous trap for anyone to get sucked into. Part of this phase is learning how to celebrate others while sticking to your own vision and goals.

The second place I see as a roadblock is burnout. I mentioned in the introduction that after a while, people have lived the lifestyle and they get burnt out. They have taken all the trips, bought all the cars, and started to question if building a team that is becoming more demanding is even worth it. If you have built a really strong foundation like we covered in the Learner phase, burnout is less likely to happen. In this next section, I will give you some key strategies to work through burnout if you are there, or how to steer clear from it altogether.

This section incorporates the knowledge you've built upon in the Applier and Operator Stages that we cover in PART I and shifts the focus to the *Promoter Stage*. This is where you begin to expand your business outside of your own application and operation.

In *The Lifestyle Phase*, we are getting into the meat and potatoes of leadership. I am going to help you with your own personal leadership blueprint that is going to help you stay focused on the goals and move yourself effortlessly into the leadership role in your business as your team starts to grow. We are also going to talk about how you can start your newest team members on this same path and keep it simple for them to grow into leadership.

*"Our intention creates our reality."*

*— Dyer*

CHAPTER 8

# THE INTENTIONAL OPERATOR

There is a story about a thief in India. He had been a thief his entire life, born to a family who had been thieves for generations. All he knew was how to take. One night, he went into a village and began to do his job, but he was quickly discovered by the villagers who chased him out with sticks and stones.

He ran into the jungle terrified that the villagers would find him. As he ran, the jungle became thick and the undergrowth tore and pulled at his clothing until pretty soon he was running naked through the jungle. When he finally outran the villagers, he was far away from civilization. Night fell and he dropped to the ground naked, completely exhausted, and fell fast asleep not knowing what would happen to him in the morning.

At the same time, a group of spiritual seekers from another village heard that this jungle had very powerful spiritual leaders that lived there. The spiritual seekers went to the jungle to see if they could find a spiritual leader to answer their most precious question. As they moved through the jungle, they happened upon the sleeping thief. The seekers quietly put down their bags of gold and sat respectfully, waiting for the man they thought was a spiritual leader they had been searching for, to wake up.

After a couple of days, the thief finally wakes up and when he sees the villagers sitting there, he thinks he's done for. The thief thinks these are the villagers that he stole from. The first words out of the thief's mouth were, "You found me!" and they responded, "Thank God, we have been searching and searching for you." The thief says: "I know."

The thief thinks he has been found out and will be killed by these villagers. The seekers think they have found a spiritual leader to follow and answer their most precious question.

When the spiritual seekers hear the thief say that he has been waiting for them, they are convinced he is their guru. They believe he knows they have been searching for him. They tell him they have brought all of their earthly wealth and ask him for a meditation in exchange. He looks around and realizes that these are not the villagers here to kill him, but in fact a group of spiritual seekers. The thief eyes all the bags of gold and things, "Hmmm, a meditation won't be hard to make up."

For his entire life, this man has only known how to take, so he says, "Okay, here is what you do. Heaven is up there and you're down here. If you want God, you have got to take God. You just reach up and grab and pull. Don't stop doing this until he appears." The thief grabs the gold and sets off into the jungle.

The spiritual seekers believe they have gotten sound spiritual advice from the most spiritual man living, and so they sit in one-pointed devotion, reaching for God as they meditate on Him. Pretty soon things start to become disrupted in heaven, and the angels come down and tell the seekers that they must be quiet, or they will disrupt God. But they don't care, they don't want angels, they want God, so they keep on doing what the thief told them to do.

God hears them and He appears before them. The villagers stop and stare at God, and they realize that the guru they found was perfect. The meditation that he gave them was perfect. But what was really perfect? Their trust, and their intention. Whenever you commit, trust, and set your intention you can drop old beliefs and programming you have had your entire life and you can operate in a different way.

This story is the perfect example of what an operating leader does. In this phase of leadership, you must drop old programming and operate from intention. I have watched people get resentful and question their companies and leaders in this phase. They stop seeking intention and belief and start operating from entitlement and greed. The seekers in the story didn't just believe. They got into action. They had the belief behind the action and didn't stop until they got what they came for. They didn't judge what they saw, they chose to believe and go all in on what they came for.

I know some of you are fighting some old stories and programs that you have had for a long time. We all have to take accountability for our lives. Stop patterns that are self-sabotaging and live from a place of intention. It doesn't matter if you grew up in the worst part of town and have a third-grade education. You can absolutely live however you choose. But you must live with intention and drop your old programming.

# READY TO FLY

I remember when I first started, I had a very small team. I would defer everything to my upline leader because I didn't feel capable and competent to lead even a couple of people. I was willing to do whatever he said, but I felt like I couldn't take any action without first having his approval to move ahead.

After the first thirty days of business and building my team, my leader kicked me out of the nest. He said, "Look, I'll jump on, and I'll help you, but I've been helping for a month. You know exactly what it takes to build this business." My mentor knew that I was ready to fly. He pushed me very quickly because he wanted to empower me to become a leader. This doesn't work for everyone! You have got to know your team and people as you start to become a leader. But, you will want every single one of your leaders to learn how to fly. You don't want to create a nest full of leaders that need you to do everything for them or get your approval on everything.

When I got kicked out of the nest, my leader knew I could learn to fly. He had already trained me, guided me, and he knew what my skill set was. It became very apparent to me quickly that I had to become very intentional about how I was operating in my business. I didn't have my leader to spoon-feed me anymore.

My leader pushed me to do things like leading group calls, leading group presentations, and being the expert in three-way conversations. When I look back, I cringe at how bad I was. But my leader was intentional about how he was training me to operate in business. He knew I had to be bad, so that I could learn how to fly on my own.

After a month of letting me spread my wings, he had me create my own training. Now the training wasn't very long. They were only fifteen minutes, but he had me create my own training once a week for my team. Just like he told me, he wanted me to start operating like a leader and not look to him for everything. I remember that he would hop on to listen and then afterwards he gave me direct and to the point feedback. One time after a call I realized what he was doing.

# MOLDING YOU FOR THE FUTURE

He was taking a leader of followers and molding me into becoming a leader of leaders. He was giving me feedback for myself, but he was also teaching me a framework that I could use as I started to have emerging leaders come up in my business. He was molding me into the future version of myself that he believed I could be. This changed everything for me! I wanted to operate in the vision that my leader had for me. I wanted to be a leader of leaders. I wanted to be the mentor that he had been for me to someone else! That changed everything for me when I started to see the vision of stepping into the role of mentor for someone else.

At this point, I knew I wasn't a great speaker or trainer, but I was committed to the process. I was committed to being intentional in operating from the vision I was creating. I knew that I was beginning to become a leader. At this point, you may think that I went out and created huge success and never looked back. Wrong.

The opposite happened. When I grew in my vision, limiting beliefs, imposter syndrome, and self-sabotage kicked into overdrive, and I started to falter. Why was it that right when I saw myself as a leader I started to struggle so much with my mindset? Years ago, I learned that new levels bring new devils. That was 100% true with me. I had just unlocked a new level of belief! And of course, a new brand of devil came out to play.

Michelangelo is one of the most famous sculptors and painters of all time. When asked about his work "The Statue of David" Michelangelo said, "Every block of stone has a statue inside it, and it is the task of the sculptor to discover it." That is our job. We are all blocks with statues and greatness inside of us. I truly believe that. But I think that so many people get stuck as blocks because of fear. Michelangelo was no stranger to fear. He battled fear of failure often. He didn't let fear stand in his way. I talk all about how to overcome the major fears in network marketing in my book *The Game of Conquering*. Don't allow fears and limiting beliefs to hold you back.

If any of you are fans of the original Mario Brothers, maybe you can relate to seeing the antagonist, a character called Bowser, at the end of levels of the game. You have to battle and defeat Bowser to move forward. The big trick is that at the end of each level he gets different powers. You never know what version of Bowser you are going to be facing. In network marketing, this is called "new level, new devil."

I almost let my fear stop me from becoming what I was meant to be. I felt like I had just had a huge win with my mentor when suddenly it felt like a HUGE new devil came out to try and fight me. Just when I was ready to celebrate, an obstacle blindsided me and I wasn't sure what to do next.

My self-talk became very fear-based. I was scared of other people's opinions. I was fearful of rejection. I was afraid I would lose the customers and builders I had just worked so hard to get. The fear became so real that my wife even started to see it was impacting me in my personal life as well. Anytime we would go out with new people, I would get anxious and worry that they wouldn't like me. I started to have social anxiety like crazy. New levels, new devils my friends. I tell you all of this because I want you to know that I see you. I see that at this stage of leadership you have hit obstacles, fears, and struggles. No one goes into the battle of business without getting some scars. You don't have to quit. You don't have to feel like you are alone. You don't have to be afraid to speak your fears out loud. You are with a warrior of other network marketers that are here to strengthen you as you build your business and your leadership skills.

I can't tell you the number of times I have been hosting high-level mastermind events and someone will raise their hand and say something like, "I can't believe I am admitting this, but I am struggling." They go on to mention what it is they are struggling with and that they are sure that no one else is going through it. They get embarrassed for being a multimillion-dollar earner and still struggling. Time and again they are blown away when the room erupts with "I have been there" or "I am struggling with that too." Leadership doesn't mean being bulletproof. It means that we are willing to see the weaknesses and obstacles and come up with solutions to solve it. Going back to the game Mario Brothers, that is how every single kid I knew ended up defeating all of the different versions of Bowser. We would get together and talk about what worked and didn't. We would share our insights and help each other out.

As you move into becoming an intentional operator, some of the work you will need to do is look at your plan for intentionally overcoming the new devils. Don't let the new obstacles stall you out. If you find that your new devil is the same as mine was at this level of leadership, find others that are there or have been there before. Seek guidance like we talked about in the learning phase of leadership. You can also listen to or read my book, *The Game of Conquering*. I share the exact strategies that I implemented to get over my own fears that were holding me back.

As I started to look at why these fears came up and what I could do about them, I finally realized that my goals and my dreams were bigger than my fears. I knew I would conquer the fears no matter what it took. I knew I would commit to making myself better and working hard on my mindset. But let me be clear, there were days where I would allow my fears to beat out my dreams. But overall, I started operating intentionally and calling myself out when I saw it happen. I allowed my dreams to beat out my fears.

Network marketing is one of the best mirrors for self-reflection that I know of. You get to face all your weaknesses, fears, and worries as you step into network marketing. But, here is the part that not many people talk about. Everything in the mirror can be changed. There is not one fear or worry that you can't overcome. I promise you that. If you are willing to be honest with yourself, see the weaknesses, and not make them mean anything, you can get over them.

I saw my fears. I saw my lack of confidence with public speaking. I recognized my doubt about leading a team. I didn't make it mean anything about me. I told myself I could learn anything. I told myself I could be nervous and excited. I could be unsure and open. I looked at the scariest parts of network marketing for myself and knew I would be able to conquer them.

I knew my leader had probably been here before too, and he had conquered his own fears in order to get to success. This is what all great leaders have to do.

As you step into a new level of leadership, I want you to remember that leaders at this new level are all going through fears of their own. They have new devils that they are battling just like you will. It is not the fear that you have to worry about. It is how you will move through the fear and conquer it that will show if you are willing to continue. It is also important to know that leaders show up WHILE they are figuring out how to conquer their hardships and fears. Leadership does not mean that you have to have it all figured out. Leadership means that you lead from the front while figuring it out for yourself. Think back on the quote that I shared with you in the beginning of this book by John C Maxwell: "A leader knows the way, goes the way, and shows the way." Leaders are always IN PROCESS. But you have to be willing to face the new devils and conquer your own fears in order to intentionally show up and operate from the best place.

# THE RESULTS ARE IN THE LEADERSHIP

When I was growing into my new level of leadership, I knew that it would eventually lead to me getting paid more. Leadership always leads to pay raises in network marketing. "Compensation always catches up to skill set and effort, but it is almost always MASSIVELY delayed." This is a post I make often on social media, and it is a good reminder that your leadership skills may be growing but give your compensation time to catch up. In the beginning of the lifestyle phase, you need to give your compensation time to catch up to all of the growth you have personally been experiencing. Patience and sticking to the foundational skills are key here. This is one piece of advice that I was given long ago. You can operate from exactly where you are right now, as long as you are willing to grow tomorrow. Intentional growth will be a superpower as you grow a team. They will see your dedication to growth and commitment to the team and the company and that will breed other leaders that follow in your footsteps.

I want you to think about how you can intentionally create an operating plan in your business. How are you going to show up when obstacles are placed in your way? How are you going to face the new levels and new devils and see that it doesn't mean anything about you?

Think back about those spiritual seekers in India. They had trust in the process. It didn't matter that the advice came from a thief. It was completely based on the trust and intention the spiritual seekers had in their own hearts.

One of the adversities I see some leaders face is that they don't have an upline that has made it to this phase of leadership. They start to tell themselves that they can't do it, because they don't have someone that can help them along their way. Some people even have uplines that have quit, and they think they have no one to turn to for help. This is not the case. To become an operating leader, you can start to see how others operate and use this example to guide you. You can also get yourself a coach. I had one woman invest in coaching, because every single person above her wasn't active in the company. She didn't let that hold her back. She set her intention and trusted the process of coaching. She became the leader that she wished she would have had in the company.

What is your intention as you grow your business? How are you going to become the leader that you want to be? Another place I want you to look at your intention is in your daily methods of operations. This is key to growing in network marketing. If you are reading this phase of leadership, you should know what a daily method of operation or DMO is. This is a great time to look at your intention behind your DMOs. Most of the time when leaders move into phase three, I ask them WHY they are doing certain things in their business. Most often they can't remember. As you move into an intentional operator, I want you to take the time to get intention around all your actions in your business.

It is time to evaluate and become clear about your business practices. You may keep the exact same systems and processes in place. That is great! You know how much I love to keep it simple. But I want you to do it from a place of intention. Just like the spiritual seekers in India, you can keep your process simple, but have the trust and intention behind it.

## What you can do right now to work on being an intentional operator:

- Remind yourself where you started and why you have kept going.

- Set the intention for your business today, it has probably changed from when you started.

- Know that new levels come with new devils—come up with a solution plan.

- Face fears head-on—don't let them stall you.

- Evaluate all your systems and practices in your business.

*"Without hustle, talent
will only carry you so far."*

*— Gary Vaynerchuk*

CHAPTER 9

# THE HUSTLING OPERATOR

S arah Blakely, the inventor of Spanx, is the world's youngest female self-made billionaire. When Sarah first thought up the idea of Spanx, she took her entire life savings, five thousand dollars, and did her research, bought the Spanx trademark, and started selling the product out of her apartment. She was hustling all day and night. She would stay up most evenings and package her product, and then in the morning would take it down to ship across the country to her raving fans. In the first year, Spanx made four million dollars.

Sarah wrote on an Instagram post, "The difference between people who achieve their dreams, and those who don't, is simple. It's about ACTION."

She went on to say, "I could have easily sat back and continued to say . . . 'one day.'" Blakely writes, "I could have kept dreaming, hoping, and wishing. But instead, I started doing, and one day became day one, 20 years ago."

Sarah started out as a woman who was selling fax machines. Spanx wasn't a family empire or something that was gifted to her. The Spanx empire was created from an idea, and hustle. Often I hear people use the excuse that someone else has more experience, more of a network, or more opportunity and that is why they are successful. Sarah was in her twenties when she started Spanx. Nothing was given to her, and she hustled and worked through every single phase of her business. She didn't let mind drama hold her back.

As a hustling operator, you are learning how to get into massive action. You know how to make money. At this point in your business, you are making over ten thousand dollars in your business. You know how to follow systems and you can obviously sell. Massive action sounds easy to some people. These are the go-getters. They know their work ethic is strong. But before you go out and do "all the things" you are going to want to take a look at tip #6 in this chapter.

This can also be the stage of business where people think that they have graduated. They think they have graduated from their DMOs (we just talked about this in the last chapter). They get away from networking. They get into management mode. As a hustling operator, you will always be sharpening the saw of hustle and work. At this stage of your business, you will be taking massive action doing things in your business that you know make you money. You will also be learning how to take risks, and step outside the box of what your mentor has taught you.

In *The Game of Networking*, I talk all about the art of networking. It never stops! You should always be networking and working your business. I once heard someone say, "People think they can stop working when they have made it in their business. That is the exact time to keep working in your business."

# BURNOUT AND YOUR BUSINESS

I had a couple come to a mastermind. They shared with the group that they had reached one hundred thousand dollars a year and they went out and celebrated. They may have gone overboard in their celebrations. They spent the next two months in "celebration" mode while completely ignoring their business. When they decided to get back to work, some of their customers had stopped ordering, and they had a couple of very frustrated business builders. Those relationships were never saved because their builders lost trust that the couple was there for them.

There is a fine line in the business of hustle, celebrating, and resetting. As a leader of followers, you will need to become more aware of when to push and when to relax. You are the greatest asset in your business. The bigger the leader you become, the more people that are going to want your time and energy.

Burnout happens to every single person I know in network marketing. I always say, if you haven't gone through this yet, that means you haven't been in the industry long enough!

It's important for every single one of you to understand exactly what I've learned from experiencing this firsthand with what I've gone through and also how I have helped countless coaching clients go through it too. I want to help you understand burnout so that you can utilize the tools yourself and be ready for when burnout comes to call in your life.

You also need to know about burnout and the signs of it so that you can help your own team members through it and teach them how to navigate it. That is what great leaders do! Burnout is a topic that many leaders don't like to talk about with their team. They are afraid that if they talk about their own personal burnout, their team will make it mean that the leader is tired of the team, or that they are thinking about quitting. They also worry that talking about burnout will lead to more people experiencing burnout. The truth happens to be the exact opposite. The more we are open and honest with the team, the more we can move past burnout and make it a more acceptable phase that we all experience.

Burnout has a lot to do with how we have been operating in our business and nothing to do with our team. It can be so difficult to lead a team, whether you're leading a small team or a big team. There are different types of burnouts. We can go through personal burnout, team burnout, company burnout, or network marketing burnout.

Regardless of what type of burnout you may experience, it can be very difficult because you don't want to fake it. You want to authentically lead, but also not be a downer for your team. A hustling operator knows themselves and is starting to learn what they can do to relax and reset.

# SEVEN TIPS TO AVOID BURNOUT

I have seven tips I teach to all my personal coaching clients going through burnout that I want to share with you. Now, you may be thinking, "Why is all of this talk about burnout happening in the hustling chapter of the book?" Because hustling the wrong way is what leads to burnout! You can't operate as a leader that your team looks up to in this phase if you are completely burned out. You can't be the leader that no one comes to because you complain all of the time about being stressed out, overwhelmed, and a hot mess. It doesn't work that way at this level of leadership. In order to be a hustling operating leader, you must learn the signs of burnout, and use these seven tips to get yourself out of it because there is no way of faking that you aren't burnt out! People can sense your energy or lack thereof.

**Tip #1 Check your belief.** What is your belief in your products, your company, network marketing, and yourself?

If you don't believe in the product, it is going to lead to burnout because you won't like talking about what you are selling. You may get resentful or hold yourself back.

If you don't believe anymore in your company, the same thing will happen. You have got to dig deep and figure out why you are with the company you are with. You have to choose on purpose to stay with them and find the good. If you don't believe in your company, you will start to see it hold you back. The same thing goes for your belief in network marketing as a profession. If you don't hold a good belief about network marketing, you will burn yourself out quickly!

Last, look at your belief in yourself. I have talked about this before, but it comes up a lot when I hear people talk about burnout. They burn themselves out because they don't believe in themselves. It is a form of self-sabotage! If you find any of these beliefs lacking, do the work to figure out what is going on and fix it right now. There is no reason to lay the path of burnout and walk down it.

**Tip #2 This is actually a tip and a BONUS tip.** Your perspective and gratitude can shift everything. First, perspective can change everything both literally and figuratively. You can shift your perspective. Here is an exercise that you can try right now. Think about where your life is right now. Now imagine what your life would look like if it were five times worse than it is right now. Write it down.

Look over what you have written and ask yourself, "If my life were five times worse, how would I still be grateful for what I had in my life?"

This exercise sounds crazy but it's all perspective. This is how I help myself find gratitude in whatever circumstances I am facing right now. Whenever you have a massive trial, you can find gratitude through anything you are going through. And I want to mention that I know there are terrible and horrible circumstances that many of you are facing. I have coached enough people to know that many people in network marketing have been through the darkest scariest experiences. This is not to discount anyone's struggles, but it is to help shift perspective and find the light in the darkness of struggle and burnout. If you have a terrible perspective on your business, the industry, or yourself, it's time to get a new perspective.

Perspective is everything. I can't tell you how many top earners I've spoken to that are bummed out because their perspective is skewed. I was speaking with a top earner and his sales had gone down by twenty percent in the last couple of months. He was totally bummed out. I asked him, "Four years ago, if I would have told you that you would be making the amount of money you are today, working from home, what would you think?" He told me, "I would have been ecstatic! My mind would have been blown!" All he is seeing is the amount he supposedly lost the last couple of months. He wasn't looking at the overall perspective. If you are struggling with burnout, how can you change your perspective?

Second, let's talk about gratitude. Gratitude wins every single time. Another way I like to gain perspective is by writing one whole page of gratitude every single day. I've done this several times with teams that I've personally coached where we go and do a gratitude blitz. I will have the team go an entire week writing down fifty things they're grateful for. I usually require twenty-five of those items on their gratitude list to be business-related. This makes people dig really deep into gratitude and think about their business in a certain way. The mind can only hold one thought at a time, and so when we focus on gratitude for an entire week like this, it can shift an entire team's perspective.

When you start focusing on gratitude, it changes everything. As Tony Robbins says, "Trade those expectations for appreciation."

Here is a quick perspective shift. Did you know that you currently have more than kings and queens did in the medieval times? Think about that. You most likely have clean drinking water, plumbing, electricity, and access to quick transportation. Many of us have much more than that. We have access to TV, cell phones, Wi-Fi, beds, homes, and the list goes on. Perspective can change everything. You are living better than kings and queens right now!

**Tip #3 Your environment will make or break you.** If you're burnt out, look at your surroundings. What's your environment? Environment is going to make a huge difference in how you are feeling. So, look around you at different areas. Who are you surrounding yourself with? What type of influences are you letting into your life? What type of products, food, etc., are you putting into your body?

One of the first areas I look at when I start to feel burnout is social media. I block and unfriend people that aren't adding to my life. I have become very deliberate online because who I see and what I read and listen to are some of the fastest ways I have felt burnout in the past. I love being online and connecting with so many amazing people, but you can find both types of energies online. Make sure you are connecting with people that are uplifting and not draining you. This works offline too. Take a look at the people you spend the most time around. Do you find yourself drained or uplifted by who you are hanging around?

I was joking around with the people at my last Breakthrough Mastermind that everyone seemed so much more upbeat and relaxed than when I see them on Zoom calls! I host many breakthrough Masterminds up at Sundance, Utah. It is a beautiful place up in the mountains, and there really is something special about being surrounded by nature and being able to relax. You don't need a mountain retreat in order to recover from burnout, but you do need to take a serious look at your environment and figure out what isn't serving you anymore.

## Tip #4 Release what you can by doing the things you love outside of your business.

I often ask my clients, "What do you love to do outside network marketing?" I can tell you one thing; network marketers are passionate! Most of us have things we LOVE that we do with family and friends outside of the business. But sometimes, we stop taking the time to do them. The business starts to take more and more of our time. (More about this in tip #7!) You have to find that passion in something outside of the business, and then make time to go and do it.

When I had a network marketing team, I would always go see a movie as soon as the end of the month was done. It was my way of celebrating and also having something mindless that I could go and enjoy and not think about numbers, sales, and team members. I also realized early on that date night was going to be huge for me to connect with my wife and disconnect from work. Where is your passion and excitement outside of the business? You are working hard in your business. Don't lose perspective of WHY you are working so hard. Sometimes you become so obsessed with your business. I get it! I have absolutely been there. But it can actually lead to burnout because you're never taking breaks. You are always working, even though many times you aren't being very effective.

One of the best ways I have found to know when I am personally struggling with burnout is to look at time with my family. If I start to tell myself that I can't go to tennis matches, or I start to push back on family vacations and date nights, I know that I am hustling and on my way to burnout. When I start to have thoughts that I am too busy for family life, I need a reset. Know what you love and make time for it outside of business. It is all about focus. Sure, sometimes you are all out obsessed with your business as you should be. That business is building your dreams but to avoid burnout make sure you schedule out the most important things in your life. Don't go chasing the business so much that you end up losing the reason you were chasing it.

**Tip #5 Personal development all the time!** I have read over eight hundred books in the past ten years. Today, right before I started writing this chapter, I spent an hour and a half focused on personal development. I haven't missed a single day of personal development in the past ten years. Why? Because I know that what you focus on grows.

One big thing that I see causes burnout is stagnation. When we get too comfortable doing the same things over and over again, we can start to feel burnout. One of the things we can do to combat this type of burnout is a massive shift in action. You can take massive action and get energized again by the business. Sometimes you can't think your way into motivation again. You've got to act your way into it. People get stagnant in their own personal growth. At this point in your business and leadership, you are seeing success. Some of you may be coasting right now. Where do you think that is going to lead you? You have to be investing in yourself all the time.

Personal development isn't something we invest in once and get returns for the rest of our lives. You must be making consistent daily investments in your personal development. I want to be SUPER clear about what I mean by personal development. We talked about this in the first phase of leadership. You have to stick to the LALA approach. Listen, Apply, Learn, Action.

It's absolutely critical that you're applying and taking action in what you have listened to and learned.

## Tip #6 Massive action is not supposed to be consistent.

WHAT?! I know, you may have to read that tip again. Massive action is not consistent. It can't be. Remember how we are talking about burnout. I see people have physical symptoms of burnout all the time. I was working with someone who ended up in the hospital. The doctor sat with her and spoke very frankly about pushing too hard too much in her business. He told her if she kept it up, she may kill herself from hustle and burnout. I love massive action. It is one of the best ways to move our business forward. But you have to imagine massive action like a faucet. You need to be able to turn it on AND turn it off. When you are looking at taking massive action, make a plan. Know when it will start, what you will be doing and also when you will stop and how you will take care of yourself during and after massive action.

**Tip #7 Build boundaries!** Draw them with a big, thick sharpie if you have to. This is a huge one. I often have people ask, "What does building boundaries actually look like?" Sometimes we make ourselves too available for everyone at all times, and that causes burnout. You don't get focused on the income-producing activities because you are doing everything for everyone on the team. I get it! As a recovering people pleaser, I have been there. At this point in leadership, you have a team. How cool is that? But you aren't supposed to do everything for them. You shouldn't be risking your health, relationships, or personal goals to help someone else build a business.

In the beginning of our businesses, we don't build boundaries and we're available for everyone at any time. I think it is because we are so excited to have them! But it's not sustainable and no business runs that way.

The number one income-producing activity is talking to new people. We all know that. It is the best way to grow and duplicate. You have got to set boundaries around your own personal income-producing activities. And if you're reaching out to new people, no one else should be able to get a hold of you. Not your team, maybe not even your family. As an operating leader, you are going to have to decide what that looks like but at this phase, you have to set boundaries.

If you don't set boundaries in your business, you will become a firefighter. The firefighter is always reacting. You want to be the architect of your life. You need to design the life you want to live in, and that includes designing boundaries that ensure that you get what you want out of your life.

Yesterday, I went through two different times where I was in all-out work mode. I didn't check any Facebook notifications, Instagram, or emails. I didn't take any calls or use my phone at all during those times. Wherever you are, be there. I've created boundaries for my business so that I am deliberately spending time on things that are important to me.

# TAKE ACTION . . . AND BREAKS!

This is one of the biggest reasons I created the network marketing planner. I wanted to make sure that network marketers could schedule their time, take action, and also take breaks! Take time off when it's dinner, turn off your phone, and log out of social media. Pick specific times in your schedule when you're working and also when you're not working. Find activities or hobbies that you feel can help you release. You can release a lot of stress and anxiety through activities and hobbies that you are interested in. The planner is a great way to start to set boundaries. You can put in the things that matter most to you and grow your business, and then see what else is available for others.

Some days you are not going to really be feeling up to it, but you can commit to action and go all in into taking action in a different way. I had this happen while I was growing. I was getting burnt out by leading a group of leaders. I had spent a lot of my time training and was feeling the burnout creeping in. I knew if I took massive action and went out and did some prospecting, I would feel energized. I spent a whole day reaching out to brand new people and had five new people join my business. Burnout went completely away, and I felt energized! If your action right now is feeling tiresome, change it up.

At this point, you know how to hustle. In this phase of leadership, you know how to make money and you are making it consistently. This looks different for different people in this phase. Maybe you have just started to make $10k. Maybe you are rank advancing and seeing bigger paychecks coming in. It doesn't matter where you are, but what matters is that you are learning that it isn't your hustle or overworking that is creating success. I remember guys in my company that would brag about the hustle. "I put in eighty hours this week!" Believe me, I have been there before, but it is not a space that we want to operate from all of the time. As an operating leader, you are moving out of the hustle 24/7 you needed when you started out. As a leader in this phase, you are working on the skill of intentionally hustling at the right time and learning how to take care of yourself so you don't get burnt out.

A hustling operator knows what to do, and what NOT to do. I have mentioned burnout and cutting things out of your life that aren't serving you. That is the definition of the hustle. The hustle means that we are putting a concentrated effort into the things that will bring you the most benefit. At this point in your business, you need to ask yourself, "What is bringing me the most benefit?" Maybe it is training your team in their IPAs (Income Producing Activities). Maybe it is finding other business builders.

Be the hustling operator that knows what to spend your energy on and what to let go. Remember the vast majority of even leaders could spend half the time they do now working and get just as much done if they just FOCUSED more. Don't confuse being busy with being productive or it will burn you out quickly.

## What you can do right now to work on being a hustling operator:

- Sharpen the skills that you have been learning. Get good at not only executing IPAs but also in teaching them to others.

- Always be working on your beliefs.

- Know where to be taking massive action.

- Be intentional about your environment.

*"The only thing worse than training employees and losing them is to not train them and keep them."*

*— Zig Ziglar*

# CHAPTER 10

# THE TRAINING OPERATOR

Tony Robbins has been called the most confident man on earth. We know that confidence isn't something you are born with. It is an intentional craft that you cultivate and work on, and Tony is the master of his craft. Tony has said, "There are always two businesses you've got to manage. There's the business you're in, and the business you're becoming. If you just manage the business you're in, you're going to get knocked out by a new technology or new competition. But if you're constantly managing those two businesses, you won't have to quit or pivot, because you're always doing something to innovate, or to change, or to improve."

Tony is always training, mentoring, and coaching. But he also spends his time cultivating, innovating, and improving his own personal life. He knows that he can't spend his time just teaching in his seminars. He has to spend dedicated time in his own personal life working on himself.

Tony Robbins trains people to be confident. He also cultivates his own training regime to continue to create confidence in himself. His mornings begin with a dip in a 57-degree plunge pool. He jumps up and down on a mini trampoline before he goes onstage. He spends retreats in the jungle jumping off bridges and facing poisonous snakes—all so he can work on his mindset and confidence.

Lucky for you and me we don't need bridge diving and poisonous snakes to cultivate confidence. But we do need to train ourselves and spend time always working on our own personal development.

# ALWAYS BE TRAINING

As a training operator you must be training others, but also you have to continue your own training. When Navy Seals are in training, they train twenty hours a day while only sleeping four hours a night. Once they have graduated from basic training their training doesn't stop. It is far from over. In fact, their training will continue for their entire time as a Navy Seal.

Unfortunately, I have seen some people in network marketing think that they have "made it."

They think they have graduated from training. They stop going to company events because they know everything. They stop doing self-improvement because they are making six figures and think, "I'm good!" It is tragic! Can you imagine a Navy Seal telling his team that he is all good to go out on a mission because he trained last year? It would NEVER happen. He wouldn't qualify to be there, because he hadn't put in the continuous effort and training into his craft.

We are always training in network marketing. We are training in our craft, and we are training in personal development. Navy Seals aren't allowed to just come to group training. They have to meet personal requirements in their mental, physical, and emotional health in order to qualify for missions. It is the same in network marketing. That is why I love the term "training operator." You will be operating a business, training others how to do the business, and you yourself will continue your training.

146

As a leader, people will always look to you to be the example. I told you in the Learner phase of leadership that people are watching you. They are now more than ever. People are looking to you to see how you operate and what you do. You can't come into network marketing with the old saying: "Do as I say, not as I do." It doesn't work that way! I mentioned this before, but it is one of the keys of leadership. Leaders are those who lead by example.

One of the first things a training operator does is look at your schedule and start to use a calendar to be efficient with your time. By this time, you may be sick of hearing me talk about your schedule. But I really can't stress this enough. One of the biggest struggles top leaders talk about is their struggle with time. They got into this business to create time freedom, but the bigger their team becomes, the more time they feel they need to spend in the business.

I often hear people say, "I just don't have the time!" We all have twenty four hours in a day. It's not the time that you are lacking. It is usually the schedule or dedication that is lacking which comes down to your vision. To be an efficient operator you must take your time more seriously and start to honor your time like you do other people's. Think about the last time you were rude and took advantage of someone's time by being late on purpose. For most of us it probably has never happened! But we do it all the time to ourselves. Why is that?

It is because we don't want other people to think badly about us. We are afraid of their judgments but are willing to completely disrespect ourselves by not sticking to our calendar, or even worse not setting up a schedule.

This past year I invested a lot of time and energy making a planner specifically for people in network marketing. It is one of my favorite tools! The goal was to make it more than just a planner. My goal was to create a community from the planner, where the community could see what works, what doesn't work, and there could be huge accountability from it. When I launched the planner, I got much more than I bargained for! People went nuts for the planner. They were excited to see something that was specific for their goals. They loved being part of a group that was all using the same tool to go after network marketing specific goals. They loved the recognition they were getting on my social media platforms.

I want you to think and write down what your number one focus for the next few months is going to be. I love to make a list of priorities, and one of my mentors reminded me the other day, "You can have priorities, but you can only focus on one." That was a huge reminder that to focus, we need to pick one thing.

So, start listing the priorities out on, and then if you want to get more deliberate at the bottom of the page and find the one thing to focus on. Once you have your one focus, I want you to write below it what drives and excites you about your goal. This is an important step and one that we already covered in the earlier steps, but remember, good leaders have vision, great leaders give vision. Even when we start to plan our time, it needs to be around the vision.

## ARE YOU EFFICIENT?

I want you to make more money. You need to get more efficient at managing your time. This includes your down time and making sure you are scheduling time that you step away from the business and be intentional about your personal time. You all know I love a good movie! But I don't plop myself down on the sofa and channel surf. Nope. That doesn't help me. I set aside time to watch movies and TV shows that I want to watch. Some days aren't going to go the exact way you thought they would, and that's okay. But having a plan allows you to get focused, and then you can map out your day with everything.

As an efficient leader, you are also going to have to be honest with your time. This goes back to having self-accountability. If you take a two-hour lunch, be honest about it. If you nap during the day, GREAT! But don't lie to yourself and your calendar by not including it. Be specific and honest about where your time is going. There is nothing worse than making the "perfect calendar" and then lying to yourself day after day and not showing up and doing the things on the calendar. You can check out my full training on planners, and how to manage your time at sperrybonus.com.

The best part is the accountability. We all know the power of accountability. As an efficient operator, you will need to be accountable. The biggest shift I see in this area of leadership is the shift to self-accountability. As you step into higher and higher ranks, money, and leadership, the accountability from others goes down. You may not have an upline that is checking in on you at the end of the month anymore. You may not have your leader getting on third-party validation calls or group chats. You will need to become more accountable to yourself than to anyone else at this stage of leadership.

I can always tell at the seven-figure masterminds who have a solid foundation of their schedule and time freedom based on how they are showing up at the event. I had one person who was texting their team, checking social media, and navigating their business all throughout the speakers. This person was feeling crunched because they didn't have support while they were gone. I asked them if they did this during personal time too. They admitted that they literally worked in all waking hours of the day, regardless of where they were and who they were with.

That is not the type of business we have all dreamed of. We talk about time freedom, but you have to be willing to get great at managing your time and sticking to what you say you are going to do. So once again, get a scheduling system and learn how to stay accountable to it!

You are also going to get really good at showing up and creating training for your team. Your team will always be in different levels of leadership and knowledge. That is one of the best and most challenging things about being in networking marketing. Part of becoming a leader is learning how to navigate this in your team.

# SPRINTERS, RUNNERS, JOGGERS, AND WALKERS

People are constantly asking me how to train their team. They have sprinters, runners, and walkers on their team, and they are all asking different questions. BUT, here is the thing you need to remember. The question will probably come up again. Someone else will start running and say, "Hey, how do I do this?" You may have just explained this to someone else. It gets exhausting at this level to get the same questions over and over again.

There is a simple solution for this. Run with the runners. Sprint with the sprinters. Jog with the joggers. Walk with the walkers. Love every single person where they are at right now, but don't feel the need to reinvent walking, running, or sprinting. As people come to you with questions and as your team grows larger, you are going to start to see a pattern in the questions that are being asked by the different groups of people. Take notes about what questions are being asked and create training answering these questions and training your team. Your goal is to create leverage from these questions. As you start to create one or two training sessions on the frequently asked questions, you will eventually have people start going to the training sessions instead of asking you for everything. This is leverage! This is what a training leader is becoming great at!

Take action in the right places, with the right people, at the right time. There is a story of a man going to work to build a dam. He spent all day by himself digging and digging. At the end of the day, he went to get paid. He told the boss, "I have created the best dam in the village." The boss said, "That may be so, but you have forgotten one thing. You built a dam on my neighbor's land, not on mine." The man didn't get paid for his hard work because he hadn't paid attention to where the work was being done.

We both know you can work. You don't get to this level of network marketing without work. But are you doing the right work in the right places for you to get to the next level of leadership? There are two places where I see people stall in network marketing. It is in the first year of business, and right around $100k in their business. So why do people stall in the operating phase of leadership? They are trying to run with walkers, and they let their sprinters take off with no leadership.

If several people have questions, you're going to go create a training based on that because rather than spending your time teaching one person, you will be creating a training on it for the group. The best part about this is that a year or two from now, you will have that training done. If anyone asks for it, you will have a specific place to direct them to instead of you having to teach that person the same thing you have taught to other team members hundreds of times.

# YOUR TRAINING BLUEPRINT

As a training operator, you will be setting up a schedule to do training. Once or twice a week schedule a training based on a specific question that someone has or a specific need that your team has right now. You can do this in your Facebook group or record it over Zoom or Vimeo. An expert tip here: if you are recording these on a social network, I recommend that you download those training sessions because you never know what will happen with the platform.

You can then take those trainings and decide if you want to utilize them on Vimeo, a website, or YouTube. Your goal as a training operator is now to start organizing the training into a table of contents. The more training you do, the more you will start to see holes in your library of training that you need to cover. This table of contents will be your guide for what you need to cover next so that you can have a complete library of training from the very start of someone's network marketing journey! Can you imagine having an entire library of training? That is exactly what you will be doing as a leader in this phase.

You can see more examples of this over on my website at robsperry. com. But think about the very newest person in network marketing. Maybe they have no idea what follow up is, so you will do a training about it. It really does start with one video and eventually turns into a very powerful library of training from the very beginning to advanced strategies. This is the best way to create that leverage because people are going to constantly have questions, and now you will have training to direct them to.

One suggestion: the more specific and better your training will be the more robust your entire system will be. I will cover more about this in the next several paragraphs. It's gonna take time to get there, but the key is, don't create so many training sessions that overwhelm people and yourself. You have the time, so schedule the training so that you can pace yourself and the team.

# CONSISTENT DELIVERY

Let's talk specifically about the presentation. Leading means there are other people involved. You will need to become consistent at delivering your message. A leader came to me and asked me to coach one of her leaders. When I asked her what she was struggling with, she said, "She is the best trainer in the world. BUT she is also the worst trainer in the world. She is the most inconsistent person in the world when it comes to delivering training. I am nervous to put her in front of anyone because I feel like she is the Dr. Jekyll and Mr. Hyde of network marketing."

This phase of leadership requires you to be consistent with your delivery. Let's go over a couple of steps that you can implement today to make sure you are showing up consistently as the best trainer you can be.

1 - Think about who you want to be and be that every single time! Do you lead from the best friend energy? Maybe you are seen more as a coach, or an expert. Pick a lane and stick to it. Being a great presenter comes from consistently showing up with the same "hat" on. So what hat are you going to pick?

2 - Practice makes perfect. You must work on your voice, eye contact, and hand gestures. Presenting doesn't come naturally for many people. That's ok! This is a skill that can be learned. I talked about this already when I was talking about my first presentation. Record your presentations and watch them back.

3 - It's not about you. Most people make presentations about themselves. They share all about their story over and over and over again. We all know that stories sell, but the story has to come back to your audience. Make sure you circle around to your audience time and time again by putting them in the story.

4 - Be the best version of you. Leadership is all about showing up even when you don't feel like it. I was watching a network marketing leader do a Facebook live. He showed up and talked about how he really didn't want to be there because he was a bit hungover from the night before. YIKES! I bet you can guess how that training went. We aren't always going to feel like training. We aren't always going to be 100 percent, but that doesn't mean that we can't get that way. You are at the operating level of leadership because you know the power your mindset has on how you show up. You know you have complete ownership of showing up and being the best version of you.

At one of my seven-figure masterminds, I had rented out this insane complex in Las Vegas called Pirates Cove. It is an epic place with several houses, multiple pools, slides, and my kids' favorite part, ice cream all day. I had set up the training to be a mix of training with some time for fun too. One evening I was playing with my kids after my training, and I whacked my head HARD trying to get ice cream for one of my kids. The next morning, I woke up with the biggest headache and a bump on my head that was visible to all!

I could have come in and told everyone that my head hurt. I could have gotten sympathy and even got a pass for a not-so-stellar training. But is that really leadership? Is that what people came to experience? No! They came to get my very best. Yes, my head hurt. Yes, I had a hard time focusing. Yes, it was a challenge to stay with my high energy. But it was 100 percent worth it. As a leader, I have trained myself to give it my all even when I don't "feel like it." I did what I could to manage the pain, I focused on the people I was there to serve, and we all had a great day with some awesome training.

As a leader, I am 100 percent capable of showing up and giving it everything even when the circumstances aren't perfect. As an operating leader, you must be able to operate under any circumstance and still perform as a leader. I talked to a leader who told me how exhausting company events are for her. She has a team of over one thousand people. When she shows up at these events, people form a line just to talk with her and get a picture with her. At first, this felt exciting to her, but she told me she is worn out from it. She decided she no longer wanted to attend events because the "fangirling" was too much. Now, I know some of you are having thoughts and maybe a bit of judgment about this. Hold on!

As a leader, you have to make those types of decisions for yourself. You have to decide what your leadership style looks like and create boundaries around how you want to show up. After I talked about this with the leader, she decided that she loved events, but she needed some boundaries. She set up times and places that she would be for different groups. She asked everyone to respect her space while she attended classes so that she could learn and take in everything that the company was teaching. It went amazing for her! She was able to engage with people in a way that felt good for her, AND still attend the event for herself and her own personal development. That is true leadership.

The next thing you will do is build boundaries. We talked about boundaries in chapter nine, tip #7. I want to give a bit more detail about boundaries because it is one of the biggest things that I coach on to help my clients reach the next level of leadership. Remember how I used to say yes to everyone and do everything? You can't operate at this level like that. You have too many people asking too many things of you. Sometimes I hear leaders say that they don't want to say no because it will make their team feel bad. That isn't going to be helpful to say yes to every single request that comes in. A lot of times we don't set boundaries and we end up always being available for everyone, every second.

# I WILL SAY IT AGAIN . . . BOUNDARIES

Boundaries help you and your team know what you expect of them, and what they can expect of you. This may seem silly, but once you set the boundary, you have to let your team know what it is. You can't get upset with everyone messaging you, calling you, texting you on the weekend if you haven't let them know the boundary. You may also need to tell them a dozen times. That's ok! It is your job to enforce the boundary.

One of my clients told me how her marriage started to suffer the bigger her business grew. She didn't set any boundaries around her time, and the team's needs kept getting in the way of family time. I asked her, "If you were to do a training on building a solid marriage while building a business, what would you train on?"

She mentioned several different things—one of them being boundaries. I told her, "GREAT! You just did an amazing training on boundaries in business and building a solid marriage. Now go and take your own advice." She did, and she was able to patch up and build a solid relationship with her husband.

I remember when the thought of leadership was one of the scariest things to me about network marketing. Leading to me meant being in the limelight and speaking to people in large groups. Leading to me meant you had to pretty much be perfect or close to it, and that scared me so much! In *The Game of Conquering*, I shared my aversion to public speaking when I was a teenager. Leading scared me so much that I almost didn't get started. I almost purposely self-sabotaged my own business because I didn't think I could be a leader.

I told myself that no amount of money would make it worth it to have to deal with the inner battle of stress and anxiety that came to my mind when I thought about speaking in public. Nowadays if you think about it, public speaking is everywhere. It is all over the different social media platforms, it is literally the life of my business.

When I started, I was extremely timid and nervous. I didn't feel ready to lead a team. I didn't feel ready for people to look to me for training and motivation. I was an expert at the tennis club, but that felt so much different than thinking about leading in network marketing. I felt comfortable and confident in my abilities to teach tennis and to help other tennis coaches. I know that some of you can relate to this. You may feel completely unprepared to lead a team, but you are just fine running your household, being a leader at church, or a manager at your current job.

Whether it was conscious or not, I knew that in order to make money in network marketing I was going to have to learn to be a leader. I knew if I really wanted to chase my goals, dreams, and aspirations, I would have to increase my leadership skills.

As an operating leader, your training never stops. Don't feel like you have to be the expert all of the time and do everything perfectly. You aren't. You have to allow yourself to learn. Remember that these leadership levels build on each other. The foundation of all leadership is learning. Cultivate your learning skills. Look at them at this level of your business and ask what else you can train in.

Training doesn't stop because you made a certain amount of money. Training is constant.

One of the things I do personally is I have a monthly mastermind with a group of people from different industries. This has made a huge impact in my life and my business. Because I am meeting with different leaders and emerging leaders from different industries, I get to have completely different takes and mindsets on topics and subjects we dive into. This group has also been a huge motivator for me and shown me what else is possible in life. I may be one of the best coaches in the industry, but that doesn't mean that my own training has stopped. That's what it means to be a leader at this level. An operating leader is always training.

On top of my monthly mastermind, I also am constantly doing my own personal development. I pick themes that I work on for my personal development experience. So, let's say I want to learn more about sleep or energy. That will be my personal development theme. I pick the topic and the amount of time I want to study it, and I go all in. If you were to look at my Audible account, you would be able to see the themes I was in based on the books I was reading at the time. Now you are learning with a focus and purpose. You will find that your ability to learn how to learn will increase dramatically with this one simple hack. Pick a theme for learning so that you are intentional and deliberate. I love being intentional about my own personal development, and also constantly training myself in different areas that are impacting my clients.

## What you can do right now to work on becoming a training operator:

- Keep up with your own training.

- Continue to get more training in areas that you are interested in.

- Start to collect frequently asked questions.

- Find a place to house the recordings of your trainings.

- See yourself as the example.

- Show up 100 percent for all of your trainings.

- Be consistent in your own personal DMOs and training with your team.

*"I'm investing in myself, I'm investing in others, and I'm investing in the cause. I know if I persist it will pay back dividends and it always does."*

*— Simon Sinek*

# CHAPTER 11

# THE INVESTING PROMOTER

"The Six Degrees of Separation" is the idea that all people are an average of six or fewer connections away from everyone else in the world. It means that if I tell you someone's name, you could probably connect yourself to them in six or less people. "My cousin's wife goes to a hairdresser who went to school with him!" You get the idea. There have been countless studies done and the conclusion has been that we are closer than we think to every single person in the world. With social media, it has gotten even easier to connect to people by seeing what friends you have in common, and I daresay that being in network marketing makes those connections get even closer! I think about how many people I coach worldwide, and it blows my mind to think about how many connections I have been able to make through this industry. It really does make the world feel connected, and I like to think that I could get connected to anyone across the globe.

In 1994, Kevin Bacon, an American actor, was being interviewed by a magazine, and he talked about how he had worked with almost everyone in Hollywood. Shortly after this, someone wrote an article called "Kevin Bacon is the Center of the Universe." The journalist took the six degrees of separation and made Kevin Bacon the topic.

After reading that, some college kids started a game called "Six Degrees of Kevin Bacon." Same theme as six degrees of separation, now they were just using Kevin Bacon as the main person to connect to. There were books, board games, and endless hours played among different groups of people around the world all talking about Kevin Bacon. Just so you know, I know Kevin Bacon through someone I introduced on stage who is a good friend of Kevin's wife.

So how does this relate to investing? At first, Kevin Bacon didn't like the game. He thought that people were making fun of him, and he wasn't on board. It wasn't until someone close to Bacon stepped in and explained what a huge compliment this was that he decided it may be a good thing for his career.

As soon as Bacon himself got behind the idea, his career took off again. Kevin started to do talk shows with the college kids that had invented the game. He started to invest in meeting more random people so that they could be more connected to him, and he started to even play the game himself with people in the movie business. He took something and decided to run with it. Kevin said that once he started to invest and promote the game, he saw a significant uptick in recognition and in his film career again. He didn't become the "has been" of the industry; he became the "must have."

# BECOMING THE "MUST HAVE"

We all want to be the "must have" in our industry, in our company, and in our team. Part of that comes from being a leader that is willing to invest. You must be able to see where the opportunity is to not only invest in yourself but invest in your team. As a leader at this level, you are working on becoming a solid leader to others. You will be supporting and training people that may even surpass you in this industry. Are you going to be sulky about it? OR are you going to embrace it? You can become a must have by how you show up for your leaders. This is a mind shift for many people. We have to shift from wanting our own success to wanting others to succeed just as much.

When I had been involved in the network marketing profession for about five years, I had finally created some credibility, had started to duplicate myself, and I had become an amazing leader of followers with an occasional leader sprinkled in. I had hit a roadblock because of my way of doing business. I hadn't really set up a plan of building leaders, I had set up a plan of being successful and needed by my team.

That was a harsh reality, but it was one that I took full ownership for. I was getting restless, and I wanted to start with a new company and build from the very start with the end in mind. I wanted to create a team that truly was all about building others and creating the best leaders in the industry. But I knew that a big part of that would be changing myself and investing in a different way of building. I couldn't show up and do all the things for all the people. If you try to be everything to everyone you will be nothing to no one.

I made a goal to become that leader of leaders. I didn't want to breed followers and do everything for everyone; I had tried that before and it didn't work! My goal was to become that leader that promoted others. I didn't want to be the one doing everything, I wanted to invest in making better leaders than myself. I wanted to create a team that really pushed me and that I could someday look up to. I set out to invest in people and work smarter, not harder.

At this point in my business. I had been working full time for five years in network marketing. When I say full time, I mean all out crazy, full-time focus. I brought on some incredible leaders from day one that I had worked with in the past, and I let them know that I would be showing up differently than I had previously.

I told them that for the first thirty days I would do anything and everything for them. I would help with everything from presentations to invites. I would help them get people in front of the tools and then teach the tools. After thirty days, those leaders were going to learn to fly! I learned this from my mentor like I mentioned in previous chapters, but I hadn't implemented it into my own team. I kept doing everything for everyone so that I could hit my own goals, and so that people liked me. Now, as a leader that was teaching my team to fly after thirty days, I told them they could leverage me for people that were interested. But, on a scale of one to ten on interest or skill set, the prospect had to be a seven or higher for me to get involved. I set boundaries. We talked about this in the last phase of leadership. I set boundaries around how I would work, who I would show up for, and what I was willing to do. It was not easy! Boundaries are never easy, especially for the person who sets them. I knew I could swoop in and do it all, but it didn't align with my vision. My focus was on building leaders, not followers.

I was deliberately setting my team up to learn first, and then jump into action quickly. I wanted to be a leader of leaders, which meant that I wanted to be constantly training up the next great leader. My vision was to create a massive team of leaders, and I knew I couldn't be doing everything for everyone if I had a large team.

## INVEST IN YOUR SYSTEMS

The investing leader invests in themselves and their own systems. The thirty-day system I just told you about probably sounds easy. It was one of the most painful things I did in network marketing! It was painful to watch people not take advantage of the help the first thirty days. It was painful to not say yes to every single request that came my way. It was painful to not step in and help when a leader called and told me that their prospect was at a level five interest. But I knew that in order to be a leader of leaders I needed to allow this process to take place. This never means to abandon team members. Instead, you create systems that take care of everyone so that you can focus on the very most important tasks.

Here is what ended up happening. As I stepped into my role as a leader of leaders, I had other teams that ended up passing me up my second month with this new business. I had leaders step up to the chance to lead their own teams. I had leaders that gave me a chance to do the business differently this time around. I had time freedom more than ever because I had built a team of leaders.

As an investing promotor you are going to be investing in the right things in your business. At this phase you are probably making between $100k–$250k annually in your business. You have people on your team, and you are growing. You and I can be honest with each other and admit that you need to be very direct about where you are investing.

You can't spread yourself too thin and invest time, money, and energy into everyone. That is one of the reasons we create training and automation for people that aren't fully committed. You don't leave them out on their own, but you also aren't spending five hours on the phone walking them through every single thing. Your time is precious. Your energy will run out, and your money can't go to everyone. You have to be willing to look at your business and ask yourself, "Where do I want to invest and how much?"

I have a friend that is a great networker. He invests in his business very intentionally. Every single year he sits down and makes an investment plan. He writes down all the places he would like to invest. He even includes things like relationships, and his health on this plan. This plan doesn't take him thirty minutes to map out; it takes him an entire day. He said, "Why would I throw money, time, and energy into things that don't give me a return? I spend so much time creating an investment strategy because I want to make sure that I get the best return possible."

Let's look at an example. Maybe you have a leader that has been with you from the very beginning. You have invested time, money, and energy into this person, but the return is really low and continues to be low. They say things like, "I am too busy." OR "If I had X then I could make it happen." They are the Debbie downers who never take action or accountability. How long are you going to invest your precious time, energy, and money in them? You already know the return is terrible! Just like I said, that doesn't mean that we cut them off, but we are honest with ourselves and invest in them the appropriate amount. As an investing promoter you are going to start to create a way to know who to invest in and how much to invest in. This goes back to knowing if people are sprinting, running, jogging, or walking in the business.

I will give you a couple of ways that I started to know what investment pool to put people in:

1 - Ask them. Most people will be honest when you ask the question, "How invested are you going to be in your business in the next thirty, sixty, and ninety days?"

2 - Look at the results. What are the numbers in the business telling you? What are their sales, what are their recruitment numbers? What is their true effort on focusing on the #1 income-producing activity which is inviting new people to look at your business or products?

3 - What does their time commitment tell you? Are they showing up for training, are they checking in with you?

4 - Look at their level of leadership. You can use this book and check out the first phase of leadership. If you see that they are working their way through the leadership phases, you may want to invest a bit more in them.

I constantly get asked, "How much should I be investing in my business?" Or "How do I create a budget for my business?" There isn't an easy answer, because everybody's at varying levels in their business, how much time they're spending in their business, and of course, how much money they have saved. You also have to consider that you still have a traditional job and what that is making you.

But here is my rule of thumb for investing in your business. Invest 10 percent back into your business consistently. For many that may seem too small at this level of leadership. Maybe you haven't created the budget, but as a leader who is now getting into the promoting phase of leadership, you will want to have an investment budget for your business.

Many people will say, "When I'm wealthy I'm going to reinvest in my business." The problem is most people that say that actually aren't wealthy and will never become wealthy. Harsh? You aren't reading this for me to flatter you. You are here to learn how to lead. Part of leading in this industry in investing. Think about the person that waits to invest in their business until they have made it. On the off chance that they do, they typically won't invest in the business then either!

# INVEST IN YOURSELF

The greatest athletes in the world invest in themselves. Many Olympic athletes have been investing in their training since they were young kids. And the investment never stops. Can you imagine someone showing up at the Olympics without a coach? The greatest investment you can ever make is in yourself. Think about it. If you fall into a scarcity mindset around investing in your business, I want to encourage you to check out my book, *The Game of Conquering*. I talk all about scarcity and how it is robbing you of your highest potential.

Let's be honest with each other. We have all struggled to invest in our businesses. I know when I first started in this business, and I was going to my first ever convention I was freaked out about the cost of everything. I didn't want to travel, pay all the money, get a hotel, pay to go to the event. I kept talking myself out of it by saying, "I can't afford this!" But I couldn't afford NOT to be there. By this phase of leadership, you are going to get really good at investing in your business. You're going to treat this like a real business. The investment is so minimal in comparison to starting a traditional small business or buying a franchise. And so, when you put that in perspective, it will help you. It also helps to increase your commitment, along with accelerating that learning curve. As a promoting leader, start thinking about where you want your investment in your business to go. In large part, the level of your commitment will determine your level of success.

Time is the most valuable thing we have on this earth. Don't ever forget that. You need to value your time and understand how precious your time is. As an investing promoter, you need to understand that when you say "yes" to anything, you're saying "no" to something else. One of my friends says, "If it's not a hell yes, it's a hell no!" And what she means is that if she says yes to something, she wants to make sure she can fully commit and be all in. If she can't, then she has got to say no so that she frees up her time for the things that she is fully committed to.

As you start understanding and really putting this into practice, it starts to help increase your focus. My number one goal this past year was to say no more often so that I could say yes to the things that mattered most. I wanted to keep the focus on the main thing, and as I did that, I found that I was able to increase my business by seventy percent.

I was working fewer hours than the previous year, and yet my revenue went up. How does that happen? By investing in the right things and saying no to the things that would take me out of alignment.

Another way to become the ultimate leader of leaders is to start investing in your business where you are at right now. I already covered with you in this chapter my formula for investing in your business. Start where you are. Don't wait and tell yourself, "When I am a million-dollar earner, then I will invest."

Right now, I want you to figure out these two numbers. The first number is: how many hours do you spend working in your network marketing business? I want the real numbers. Not the fake hours that you pretend to work that you're merely scrolling on social media, but real hours that you are doing business. I want to know the real hours that you're working on average, just estimate it. Next, I want you to figure out how much you make an hour.

Simple math here, hours worked and how much you make an hour. This can help us figure out your monthly averages for hours and money. If you want to make, for example, $300,000 a year working 25 hours a week, that means you want to get to making about $250 an hour. If you want to be a leader, then you need to start thinking like a leader. You need to start to see yourself as a leader making the money and investing strategically in the right places. Often, as we get into business for ourselves, we think about keeping all of the money for ourselves. We want the profit to be as high as we can get it! You start to do everything yourself, like that client I told you about.

But here's an example. Say you want to add an extra hour every week to your business. Let's say that means hiring someone to mow your lawn. Yes, I know for many it could be less time but let's just go for example's sake and say that it takes an hour, and let's just say it costs $35 for everything. Maybe they're doing more than just mowing your lawn every week. If you spent an hour on your business every week, that's 52 hours a year you just added to your week. Now, I want you to really think deep on this if in those 52 hours you actually focused on making new contacts in your business—meaning making brand new invites for people to look at your products or your business and you didn't waste time. Think about the difference that could make.

As a leader at this level, you have got to realize that the difference will always compound. You may say, "Yeah Rob, but I'm paying $35, and I'm only making $30/hr. right now in my business." A promoting leader thinks bigger. They understand the compound effect. They know that as they start doing the math and see that even if they spent one hour paying for lawn care, that is one hour they could be doing income-producing activities that will build over time and pay off in the long run.

If you're deliberately watching your time, you will get to the point that it will compound. Eventually that residual will compound, and it will grow and grow. Think about this, billionaires don't work harder than millionaires. Millionaires don't work harder than six-figure earners, and six-figure earners don't work harder than a lot of people that make minimum wage. Billionaires have learned how to compound their effort and invest in the right help. Understand leverage and how to pick the best way to get the most out of your time, energy, and money. We know the highest income-producing activities are talking to brand new people. If you can truly focus on doing that and outsource all of the other stuff that doesn't really need you, you are going to crush your business and take it to the next level.

# INVEST IN HELP

Let me tell you some things that I have outsourced to make sure I am investing and promoting the things that will give me the biggest returns. In my personal life, I have hired out all outside maintenance of the house—yard, cars, toys, etc. I have also hired out inside for cleaning, maintenance, and decorating. I have hired coaches to help my kids with tennis, swimming, and any other hobby they have taken an interest in.

With my business, I hire out most of the tasks for day-to-day operation. I have Facebook ads, social media people, videographers, content writers, publishers, photographers, coaches—you name it—I have hired them out in my business. I have stayed very focused on my own income-producing activities and making sure that I spend most if not all my time doing those things.

STOP! If you aren't at this level, you are not allowed to get overwhelmed. This is some next-level training to help cast a vision of where you will be someday! Be where you are at, and see the value in the future of this, but never get overwhelmed thinking that this all needs to be implemented today.

You are at the level of leadership now that you are going to need to hire help. This is an investment into your future self and leading by example. I ask some of my leaders, "Are you leading from the front?" What that means is that they need to show up and stay in the front of the action. They can't be making graphics, running the audio/visual booth, manning the camera, checking hair and makeup, AND be on stage. They have to show up and be the person on stage. Hire everything else out, and lead from the front. We are going to cover more of this in the chapters ahead, but I think it is important to start thinking about areas that you could be getting help in right now.

## What you can do right now to work on becoming an investing promoter:

- Put 10 percent of your paycheck back into your business.

- Invest in your personal growth.

- Invest in your team's growth.

- Invest in systems in your business that keep the business going.

- Work on being more deliberate in your work.

- Start investing in hiring everything else out

*"People work for money,*
*but go the extra mile for recognition,*
*praise, and reward."*

*— Dale Carnegie*

# CHAPTER 12

# THE RECOGNIZING PROMOTER

**A**braham Lincoln said: "Don't worry when you are not recognized but strive to be worthy of recognition." Lincoln did just that in his life. He was a man that is worthy of the recognition that he has had. Lincoln has been known for his communication, listening, and negotiating skills.

One of my favorite things about Abraham Lincoln is that he was an entirely self-taught man. From an early age, his parents saw that he was extremely bright. They put a huge focus on his learning and self-education. He was always found with a book in his hands or nearby. He started to be able to recite passages from memory and it had a huge impact on other people. Someone who met him as a young man remarked, "That boy will change this world." And he did.

But what drove him to become the type of person that he was? What was it that made him put himself out there over and over again? Part of it was his drive for recognition. Though he did it humbly, and was always gracious, it was a known fact that Lincoln loved to hear praise from other people.

# MEN DIE FOR IT, WOMEN CRY FOR IT

Let's think about recognition. Men die for it. Women cry for it. It is true! Really, I want you to think about it. Men die for it. Women cry for it. It is so absolutely key and critical that we understand the importance of recognition. Out of all the things I see teams fall apart for, this is the main and critical one. As leaders, we need to figure out how we contribute to our team with recognition. Everyone wants to be seen for their efforts and accomplishments.

One of the important parts of recognition is promoting others. Promoting others and recognizing them publicly does several things. First, it empowers them to step into leadership roles themselves. Second, it shows them and others that you trust them. Third, we communicate to our teams the things that we are seeing and paying attention to them. Being able to recognize and promote our team members helps us cultivate and show them how we truly feel. A huge bonus for us—the things that get recognized and noticed are the things that improve.

Many times, as leaders we get stuck in the rut of being everything to everyone. We do this for several reasons. Sometimes we ourselves need recognition and want to be the hero. Or, we haven't taken the time to train anyone else on what we do. Or we haven't taken the time to know what other people need, and so in the moment, we end up taking care of it and putting fires out. What we really need to focus on is figuring out ways we can promote others and ask others to lead out. Don't forget, you are training LEADERS! If you are following this rank advancement blueprint, you are training leaders to duplicate, leaders who are leading by example, and leaders who know the importance of all the skills we have covered in this book. You are training your resources, now start to use them.

How can you promote others in all different aspects of your business today? For some of you, it could be promoting someone right when they join the business. You can give them a shoutout and let people congratulate them on the team. It could be asking a new business builder to lead the first part of a team call. You could even show confidence in your team leaders that have been with you to help come up with the next team event.

You are all leaders. But if you want to step into being a leader of leaders, you want to help promote your team in their journeys. Promote them being the best customers, the best new builders, or the best leaders in your team. Learn how to promote what you want to see duplicated.

I know that network marketers love good competition. So here is a challenge I want to put out for you. I challenge you to find as many ways as possible to promote and recognize your team for the next two weeks. Think of everything and anything you can do to promote and recognize the newest member to your most seasoned team leader. Another idea is collaboration because people love being a part of the process. Have your top 3, 5 or 20 team members all come up with 3 different ideas to add more recognition. Then take the best recognition ideas and use them. I want to hear what you have done. Once you have done this, come over to The Game of Networking Facebook Group and post about it using the hashtag #promotingleader.

Here are some examples to get you started. You can promote them and have them lead training or part of the training. You can ask people to share their story and validate them. You can have someone share their perspective about building the business and recognize their contributions to the team. Think of all the different ways that you can celebrate them. I would list literally every single way you possibly can celebrate anyone and everyone you can in your team, and then take on the two-week challenge and go and do it! I can't wait to read about all the experiences and culture it will help create on your teams.

Recognition is one of the best ways to step into the role of leadership. You are saying that you see what other people are doing. You are taking time to pause what you are doing, and really seeing people. Recognition is how a leader can stop making it all about themselves and start leading a team and seeing how they are showing up. If we know that one of the best things we can do to keep people engaged and working is recognizing them, why is it so hard for many of us to do?

Men die for it. Women cry for it.

Recognition is so huge. People will leave their jobs because they aren't getting enough recognition. There was a study years ago about the top reasons people leave their jobs. The top five reasons were "lack of appreciation." People were also willing to make less income if their boss was really good at recognizing their accomplishments and complimenting them.

Think about how you are recognizing your team. On a scale of one to ten, how do you think you are doing at recognizing people? I have every single one of my clients look at their recognition of their team. A lot of leaders think that they're really good at it, but when we start to dissect their recognition plan, they always find things to do to improve it. It doesn't matter if you have been in the business for one month or thirty years, we can all get better at giving recognition.

# PROMOTE WHAT YOU VALUE

If you are passionate about humanitarian efforts in your company, but you don't recognize it in your team, marketing, and brand, then essentially what you are saying is that it isn't important enough to mention. You can talk all you want about how important something is, but if you're not recognizing it then it isn't important to you. As a leader, you will know the difference between talking and recognizing. Like the old saying goes: "Talk is cheap." You all know how important my marriage is to me. It would be one thing for me to talk about date nights and taking time for my wife. But what does recognizing it look like? That means I am going to make time, I am going to spend time thinking and planning. I am going to make sure that when date night is happening, I am present and focused on it. That is recognition. So, are you TALKING and RECOGNIZING?

Here are a couple of ideas to help you up your recognition game. You could send personalized texts or voice messages to different people every single week. I like to do this, and I personally include it in my weekly method of operation. It has helped me stay connected and it also helps me think about people personally throughout the week. I make sure to really think about what I can recognize. It has also been great because it can be done quickly.

If weekly feels like too much, you can also schedule it monthly or around holidays. I love sending out gratitude to friends and recognizing them for their efforts and friendship during certain holidays.

You can do voice messages welcoming new members to your team. You can utilize Facebook groups by having a recognition post that everyone can contribute to. Something else you can do is switch your recognition from results to effort. Often when people are just starting out, they may not be getting a ton of results yet. That doesn't mean that you can't give them recognition. Did they make the effort? You can start to recognize efforts like how many invites they made instead of how many people signed up or showed up. Of course, we all want results, but recognizing effort is encouraging the right human behavior that you want to see more of.

Recognizing rank is a pretty easy one, but it's still something we need to make sure we don't lose sight of. You could even do spotlight of the week on members on your team. Do you remember the start of the week at school? It would be a similar setup. Every single week, you're spotlighting someone on the team. It helps people feel special, but it also helps people get to know one another.

You can recognize birthdays by sending a personal message to them. If you have a smaller team, you can do recognition inside of your team or group page. You could also recognize work anniversaries for people on the team.

One leader I work with told me how easy it is to track work anniversaries in his back office. He pulls a list at the beginning of each month of when people signed up with him. He sends personal "work anniversary" messages and gifts based on how long they have been on the team. The entire team loves it, and they all look forward to it. He said he really didn't realize how much it meant to everyone until he missed a couple of weeks. He said, "My inbox was flooded with messages from people wanting to know if I had forgotten!" How fun that this leader has created a recognition system that is so loved that people are dying for it!

Some companies offer incentive trips and big prizes for hitting big goals and ranks, but let's be real. Only a small percentage of your team is going to qualify for these things. Don't make recognition be something only a small percentage of your team gets! Every single person on your team should be recognized.

You could create even another one anytime they sponsor for customers or distributors in a month, depending on what your emphasis or focus is, or it could be every month that they make ten new invites for customers or, you know, new distributors.

Another thing you can do, and this is my challenge for you as your team grows, is to create a small committee that brainstorms ideas to recognize and that's what they're in charge of and that committee could stay there for whatever you deem long enough. It could be three months, four months, five months, six months and then it changes out for something else. And if you don't have a big enough team that's okay get together with one or two team members and start thinking of ways you're going to start recognizing people. Don't ever take recognition lightly because it is one of the most important concepts and as you are becoming a better and better leader, as you are becoming that Ultimate Creator, you need to master the art of recognition.

The possibilities for you to start recognizing your team and creating a system around this are endless. I am sure some of you are killing it in this area of your business. We want to hear about it! Head over to my Facebook group, The Game of Networking and share with us what you do to recognize your team. We only approve the best posts so give us the good stuff!

As a recognizing promoter, you are in charge of making sure that this is happening. Don't leave it to someone else or think that the company recognition is enough. You must have a system in place that you do specifically for your team. Sadly, I have watched a top leader's team fall apart because the recognition was missing. She told me that their paychecks and company swag when they hit a rank should be enough for everyone. Slowly people started leaving and going to different teams because their leaders were recognizing them. Don't build a team just to see it crumble because you aren't willing to be a recognizable promoter.

At this phase of leadership, you are going to have some great leaders emerging from your team. Always remember that they will each time appreciate your recognition. Your leaders may start to be hitting those impressive ranks, and that is great, but that doesn't mean that your recognition stops. Be committed to reaching out and taking the time to recognize accomplishment and effort even to your very biggest leader. Recognition is key from your newest person all the way up to the highest earner.

## What you can do right now to work on being a recognizing promoter:

- Create a recognition plan. If you already have one in place, look at it with a fresh set of eyes.

- Ask mentors and team members for new ideas that have worked in recognizing others.

- Create a "recognition library" that you can pull different strategies from.

- Always be looking for ways you can offer praise. Don't make it always about the rank.

- Continue to recognize your top leaders. Your top leaders may start to have their own teams, but they still need your support and recognition. Never stop.

*"Culture is the widening
of the mind and the spirit"*

*— Jawaharlal Nehru*

# CHAPTER 13

# THE CULTURAL PROMOTER

Zappos' CEO Tony Hsieh is on the forefront of company culture. Tony said, "At Zappos we really view culture as our number one priority. We decided that if we get the culture right, most of the stuff like building a brand around delivering the very best customer service will just take care of itself."

Since the beginning of Zappos, the company has dedicated much of their time and energy to creating the company around the culture it wants to maintain. They are so dedicated to their culture that they are willing to hire and fire based on the culture, mission and values that they have set up. One of the biggest successes of their culture plan is their focus on their company being fun, happy and a bit weird. This has created die-hard consumers that are willing to stick with the company.

Zappos has also centered much of their culture around the customer's interactions and experiences with employees at Zappos. They pride themselves on authentic connections and interactions with each and every customer. They spend extra time on their calls and don't have a set time that they "should" be spending to listen and take care of their customers. Back in December of 2011, Zappos broke its personal record for the longest customer service phone call on December 8 with a conversation that lasted 10 hours and 29 minutes! The company decided early on that the culture would have service evaluations based on authentic connections rather than trying to keep customer interaction to a minimum.

The culture of Zappos is very intentional and always evolving. Tony said, "It is important to come up with core values to which you are fully committed. Once you have done that, you are well on your way to building a company culture that is in line with the brand you want to build."

# THE BIGGEST ELEPHANT IN THE ROOM

Culture is defined as "the customary beliefs, social forms, and material traits of a racial, religious, or social group." In network marketing, your culture is the distinct way of running your team and thinking about business that is based on what you intentionally want to create.

Culture is the way things are done; it's the way people interact, make decisions, and influence others. In the promoting phase of leadership, you know that your conscious and unconscious beliefs are driving decisions, behaviors, and repeated behaviors of your team and business. This is what has helped you become the leader of leaders and set up the best leadership practices.

In my book, *The Game of Conquering*, I talked about how mindset will eat skills and systems for breakfast. You could say the exact same thing about culture in network marketing. Culture is HUGE, and in the last chapter, we talked about creating a recognition system for your business. Well, recognition just so happens to be part of the culture of your business. I like to say that culture is the biggest elephant in the room. It is the thing that everyone in network marketing sees, but they aren't exactly sure how to approach the subject. Most people just let the culture of their team naturally happen, and it is a HUGE wasted opportunity. Don't let the culture of your team be the elephant in the room!

Let's put this in perspective. In the book *Start with Why*, Simon Sinek made a very strong point that the reason people go to church is because of the culture that is created. He went so far as to say that people pay to go to church! They pay in tithing money, gas money to get there, and even pay sometimes for the building, etc. People are paying for the culture that is being created by the church they are going to. In this phase of leadership, I want you to think about what culture you are creating. I know that some people get really frustrated when they have people that join, they show up for calls, events, etc., but they don't explode in the business. I love this group of people! They are big keys to help you unlock what is so great about your culture.

Think back to when you started your business in network marketing. You weren't thinking about mission, vision, values, and culture. You may have wanted to make a couple of extra bucks to pay off some debt or take the family out to dinner. The majority of network marketers don't start with a culture plan and branding strategy. As you grow in the business and leadership this will become something you will need to put some energy and effort into. The time is now to create a culture plan for your business. You have people following you. You have leaders coming up in your business. People are looking to you to show up and show up with intention. So how do you learn how to create a brand, culture plan, and core values?

# NATURAL VS. AUTHENTIC

Lucky for you, part of this has already been created! Culture starts with authenticity. It starts with who you are and how you show up. I mentioned that culture is the way things are done. I also said that you shouldn't just let culture come naturally. So how do you let it authentically happen and not naturally happen? Simple. You get clear about what is authentic to you. You start to set up systems that work for you and your team. You work on seeing the authentic and nurturing it intentionally. You have been doing things in your business for quite some time. Now it's time to be more intentional about it and do it on purpose knowing that you are creating a culture around it.

Let me give you some examples. One of my clients started her business when she had small kids at home. She attracted a lot of other young moms that were desperate to connect with other women that knew what they were going through having young kids at home. Once a week these women would get together after the kids went to bed and they would work on their businesses together while all on Zoom. They called it the "after-hours mommy party." This client had huge success creating a space where moms could learn a new business and still have kids, jobs, etc. This was part of her culture, but she didn't realize it until we started to create a culture plan for her business.

Another woman I coach is in a deep and committed relationship with the brand Louis Vuitton. She is obsessed with anything the brand comes out with, especially their bags. She decided that if anyone in her company hit a certain rank, she would give them a Louis Vuitton bag! This was part of her culture.

Culture is how you are showing up. We know at this phase of your business you have been showing up. But now I want you to do it on purpose. Show up with intention and purpose. WHY are you giving away Louis Vuitton bags? What type of culture does that create for your team? When I asked my client this, she said that she loves to give these bags to people because it is something that hasn't ever been possible for them. No one on her team ever thought they would own a real Louis Vuitton bag. She said part of her culture is showing people what is possible for their lives. THAT is showing up with intention!

Just like we talked about coming up with a recognition plan, you are going to want to intentionally build a culture plan. Often in network marketing, this is a missed step. People let their culture organically take shape, and there is nothing wrong with that, but it lacks your leadership. You may end up with a culture that you didn't want!

One of my clients was having a hard time with people following up after someone had become a customer. He couldn't figure out what was going on. He had a great system in place, and he was the king of following up himself with his own customers. He knew the value of following up with his customers as soon as they had received their product. He hadn't really focused on culture and HOW people on his team were showing up. When we started to dive into culture, he found the problem. There had been a natural culture of sticking to the system perfectly UNTIL the sale was made. Once the sale was made, everyone started checking off boxes and not following through. When he started asking people about why they weren't following the system one team member said, "All the work has been done. I made the sale. There's no need for the rest of this stuff." While my client had been off growing his business, a sloppy culture had taken hold of his team.

As a cultural promoter, I want you to take ownership of the culture that you are creating—either intentionally or unintentionally. It wasn't my client's goal to create a sloppy culture, but when we found it, he took 100% ownership of it. I want you to think of the culture in your team as part of your personal brand. I want you to be able to proudly stand with the culture of your team. Your culture plan needs to be strong. It needs to have purpose and vision behind it. You need to believe in your culture and be willing to fight for it if you have to! My client created a culture plan and since has dedicated himself to keeping the team in the culture.

One of the leaders that has come to several of my seven-figure masterminds is one of the best cultural leaders I have ever worked with. Last year I asked her why her team culture is so strong. She said, "This isn't an accident. I spend dedicated time thinking about culture and what I want it to be. If I see something that doesn't fit the culture vision I have, I don't let it near me and my team. People are drawn to work with us because I have put so much effort and thought into culture."

As you're building your business in the beginning the goal is just to make your money back. Once you do that, you think about making some spending money or paying off some bills. As you increase your goal starts to change and you think about building a large team. At this stage of leadership, you should be focused on the culture that you are going to intentionally create for your team.

# IDENTIFY YOUR CULTURE

Let's talk about culture. I was doing training for a company on culture, and someone asked a great question, "What should I include in my culture plan?" The simple answer is the one that no one wants to hear. EVERYTHING should go in your culture plan! Let me explain. Have you ever gone into a shop, and something felt off?

My kids love getting drinks from Starbucks, and I am always shocked at the sticker price for a beverage! But as I was writing this book, I took a closer look at Starbucks. What is it about the culture they have set up that makes it the number one beverage consumed around the world? Starbucks takes everything into account. Did you know that they have a store layout that has been scientifically proven to make you feel supported and will make you want to buy more? Starbucks has also gone as far as making sure that your nearest Starbucks will play the exact same music as a Starbucks a thousand miles away. They know what culture is, and they use it to their advantage. Starbucks employees are also put through one of the most intense training to help them take care of their biggest asset—the customers. Part of employee training is learning the culture plan for the company.

Starbucks has thought of everything. They have systems set up so that you get the same drink in California, New York, and Australia. Their systems have created a culture for their employees and us, the customers. As we talk about culture, I want you to think about what systems you have in place, and what type of culture that is creating.

One leader I worked with had a fun video that every single new business builder would receive. The video was of her popping out of a box with confetti and sparklers congratulating them on their new business. This set a tone for the culture that she wanted to have in her business. She wanted people to know that her team likes to party and celebrate everything. Her culture didn't stop with the video. She worked with me to create a culture plan that put the focus on celebration and fun.

Your goal is to create an incredible culture that can be built on and grow with your team. Every step of the process in your business will be infused with your culture. Training, challenges, recognition—everything will need to be looked over with your team culture in mind.

You may be reading this section and freaking out a bit, "I don't know what my culture is! I haven't ever had to do this work before!" No worries! If you are in this stage of leadership, I guarantee you have culture on your team, it may be more organic than strategic and that's ok. This is a great chance to take a look and be more thoughtful about what you want it to look like.

Focus on what you want to be leading. Do you want a culture of fun and celebration? One of my clients used to be a professional athlete. He loves the spirit of competition and was sad when his pro career ended. He thought he had to retire his competitive spirit. When we created his culture plan for his team, he infused a lot of competition. Guess what type of team members he is getting? Athletes and people that love competition. In this chapter, I have included some questions to help you start to identify your culture and how to build it intentionally.

# BUILD THE CULTURE AND THEY WILL COME

A common misconception I hear about culture is that people try to force themselves into a culture that they think other people will want. For example, one leader thought that everything needed to be about fun and partying. She was an introvert who loved to keep things intimate and personal. As she tried to build a culture around fun, she completely burnt herself out and turned some of her team away.

People build with you because you are you. Don't ever try to become something that you aren't. Build a culture that can grow with you. Don't get stuck thinking that all culture on a team needs to be a party. One leader I worked with built a culture around making family first.

This was not a party and celebration of culture by any means. They focused on acceptance and support to each team member's family dynamic. Culture is personal. Make sure as a leader you are creating a culture that you are excited to think about and create around.

In the game of networking, I talked about building a company that we built our entire company culture on random acts of kindness. This was huge for getting the right people on board and helping us create systems for the company all around our culture of kindness. We loved doing a random act of kindness blitz once a month. This created the culture of attracting the people that wanted something bigger than just the business.

Personal development must be part of your culture plan. Think about what you want your culture to be with everyone's personal development. Are you going to host a book club every month with a personal development book? Are you going to do training and accountability around personal development? All of this goes into your culture plan for your team.

Team culture is HUGE when it comes to company events. You will be a team that people are proud to be on, or one that they slink away from based on your culture. There is something about seeing other teams together that makes or breaks the culture of a team. I have talked before about people being embarrassed about their team or wishing they had joined someone else just based on company events. Be the team that people are proud to be a part of because you have spent the time and energy coming up with a culture plan. All of these things add into the culture of a place that people just want to be around. Culture isn't about spending money on shirts and swag. It is so much bigger than that. If you want to buy the swag, do it, but don't think that covers your team culture.

Once you have the culture plan in place, it is your job as a leader to promote it. This entire phase of leadership is about promoting. Promoting others, mentoring, recognizing, and promoting the culture of your team. This isn't something that you can have one training about and forget it. YOU have to be the leader that is always reminding and being an example of the culture of your team.

One of my favorite leaders starts every single call with the exact same phrase. It doesn't matter if it is a team call, three-way call, or company call. She starts off and states the culture of her team. One of the leaders who has been with her from the beginning told me, "You think I would be sick of hearing it by now, but I'm not. It gets me pumped and excited each time I hear it." This leader also happens to have one of the most rock-solid teams in the industry. Her team knows the culture, and they are 100 percent all in with it.

# CULTURE BUILDING QUESTIONS

You can start to create a team culture plan by answering some questions and getting clear about the culture you are wanting to create.

Once you have defined the culture you will want to start to think about every single system in your team. Put it next to the culture plan and see how it stacks up. How to set up your team culture plan. First, think about things that you are known for personally. Choose resources that will support your culture. Lead by promoting your culture in all interactions with your team.

What do people say about you?

What are you passionate about?

What are your ideals and beliefs?

What is your vision for the team?

Create a personal motto and a team motto.

## What you can do right now to work on being a culture promoter:

- Start to observe where the natural culture is in your business. Answer the questions found in this chapter.

- Decide if you want to keep or get rid of natural culture and set the intentional culture you want to create.

- Create your culture around your missions, vision, and values. If you don't have these yet, get them!

- Use culture to see themes for team events and infuse them into every area of your business.

- Whenever making decisions about your business or your team, ask yourself if it aligns with your culture.

- Schedule in your calendar two times a year to check in with the culture of your team. Culture is always evolving, and you want to make sure it is evolving where you want to see it go.

# TOP TEN TIPS FROM TOP LEADERS ON BEING IN THE LIFESTYLE PHASE

1 - Learn how to build relationships. It is the backbone of your business! Rate yourself and be honest about how you start and nurture relationships. Always be improving!

2 - Learn how to motivate others by learning what motivates them. Listen to other people and see how you can serve them. This includes creating a community within your team. It is going to happen whether you do it intentionally or not! So, you may as well start from the beginning and be very intentional about what your community is all about.

3 - Work on your confidence in what you are selling. If you don't have confidence in that, you can kiss your rank advancements goodbye!

4 - Learn how to look at the systems that you are using in your business. Get really good at making the system work for you, so that you can turn around and teach and duplicate it with your team.

5 - Start investing more time in your team. It doesn't matter if you have followers or one builder, start to set aside time to be with your team.

6 - Start using a time management system! If you haven't started this out yet, you need to! The more that your business builds, the more time people will want from you. If you don't have a system in place, you will wear yourself out.

7 - Part of promoting others is also getting really good at tap-rooting. Learn the skill of tap-rooting and you will never run out of contacts.

8 - Course correct quickly. You may start to get distracted by other things. Always check in and when you see you or your team blinded by the new shiny object, course correct and get back on track.

9 - Start to learn how to be in a crowd. The bigger your business grows, the bigger the events you host will become. There is a skill and art to working larger crowds. Learn! Don't get stuck working the room the same way that you would with a group of four or five people.

10 - Promote others on your team! Learn how to recognize other people. Look for ways to celebrate the action and not just the results.

11 - Learn how to lead through communication. Be open and honest, but not too open and vulnerable with everyone. Know who you are talking to, and what is appropriate to be saying in that group.

## The Legacy Phase
## $100k–and beyond

# THE 3 PHASES OF LEADERSHIP
## THE FOUR STAGES

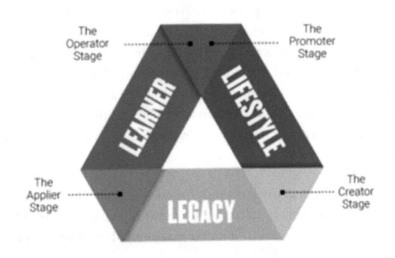

When you lead a life of legacy you are focused on the bigger picture. You start to think more about what impact you want to create, who you want to help, and where you can serve. Your focus shifts from being about you to making the biggest impact for others. This is the phase that I always dreamed of being in when I was doing network marketing. I came up with my life's mantra: "Die with memories, not dreams." To me, this meant I was at a point in my life where it wasn't about living paycheck to paycheck or even just living an epic life. In this phase, I was able to help others create memories to last a lifetime, and not die still wishing.

The legacy phase is truly about creating a legacy that you are known for. It is about reaching past your family and into communities, villages, and cultures. It is about impacting the world through your money, influence, and expertise. In this phase of leadership, you are making $100k and beyond annually. You are focusing on giving back and seeing where there are needs that you can fill.

In this phase your business is successful, and you have become a leader of leaders. You are starting to transition into the highest phase of leadership, which is mentorship. I love this phase so much because it is where I see people really start to step into service. To give you more perspective on this phase, have you ever wondered why most billionaires don't retire? Have you ever wondered why most great coaches who make millions upon millions rarely retire? They are beyond the money and the fame. Everyone finds different ways to give back. Everyone finds different ways to create a LEGACY but those with high leadership levels soon discover that creating a legacy is one of the highest forms of happiness. Creating a legacy helps one fulfill their true potential.

One of the leaders at my last mastermind was talking about how she made over a million dollars in her network marketing business the previous year. She said, "The greatest thing that came out of my business was being able to hire single moms in my area to help support and run my business. I was able to pay them wonderful salaries, work around their schedules with their kids, and set up skill retreats where I would show them exactly how to do what I was doing." She then went on to tell me that she loves when these women come and give their two weeks' notice because she knows they are going on to do bigger and better things in their lives. I checked up with her while writing this book, and I asked her if this pattern in her community is still going. She told me, "The impact that my little business has had on this area is incredible. The women here are thriving and creating their own wealth and success." That is what being a legacy leader is all about.

We transition into legacy leadership when our sole objective becomes other people and helping them. The paychecks and money that we receive are amazing, but legacy leaders truly are about serving and helping others first. In the next several chapters we are going to talk about how to become a legacy leader, some of the challenges that legacy leaders face, and how to overcome the challenges. I am going to share with you the blueprint for moving from leadership into mentorship and how to utilize the leaders on your team so that you can continue to create a mentorship role without leaving the business behind. Find a purpose much bigger than YOU.

*"Create the highest grandest vision possible for your life, because you become what you believe."*

*— Oprah*

# CHAPTER 14

# THE VISIONARY LEADER

Even though Prada had been around since 1913, it didn't become a high fashion standard until the 1980s when Miuccia Prada took control of the family business. Since taking over as CEO of Prada, Miuccia has internationally expanded the brand, acquired several other fashion brands, and even created several new lines of Prada products. The Prada name is synonymous with luxury, cutting edge, and high fashion. Prada even has raving, obsessive fans who will literally fight over the product as it hits the shelves. Miuccia said, "Every day I am thinking about change," and this definitely shows in the brand.

Miuccia is known for being a visionary of the company. She is not afraid to push past what has been done before and always is thinking about the next great idea or interesting take on fashion and products. She even took retail space to the next level with her pioneering approach to Prada stores in L.A., Tokyo, and New York. Some people in fashion are seeking to know what the next trend will be, but Prada is actually the one setting the trend.

Season after season, Miuccia is showing the vision she has for what a woman can be. She continues to be curious, asking questions about everything. She is not afraid of what others think and has a passion for what she does.

Other designers are always looking to the Prada brand to dictate what is next in the industry. Cathy Horyn, a fashion critic, said, "Prada's designs stem from an inner vision of herself."

It is Miuccia Prada's passion for creating through her visions that has made her a leading legend in fashion, and a billionaire. Prada said, "I invent people for a living. You can use clothes to reinvent yourself, and it can be one of the cheaper ways of changing yourself." I don't know if my credit card would agree that clothes are a cheaper way of changing yourself after my wife's infamous shopping spree, but I agree that clothes can change a person.

When I read about Miuccia and her ways of leading the Prada company I was struck by her all-consuming curiosity with her work and business. She has allowed herself complete freedom to create, and it hasn't always come out without a hitch or a failure. In 2015, Prada had overexpanded in the Asian market and had priced their products too high. Their strategy had tanked and was costing them a fortune.

But that didn't stop the company from reinventing themselves for the Asian market and relaunching with a new strategy in 2016. The CEO wasn't going to let failure and setbacks hold back her vision of the future of the company. When interviewed, Miuccia said, "It comes from me. It's my soul. It's my life. My work and my life are more or less the same thing, and I never consider that the work is something different. The job, the foundation, my personal life, it's all one thing." It was this vision of creation of self, work, and creativity that drove Prada forward even in the face of adversity.

# SETBACKS ARE PART OF THE PLAN

If you haven't had any setbacks, hardships, and adversity on your team yet, you haven't been around long enough! All of these are inevitable in this business. If it's not with your team, it will be with your company. If it's not your company, it will be your team! And most likely, it will be both. As a leader of a leader, you have been through adversity probably many times over.

Every single successful company in the entire world of network marketing or non-network marketing has had adversity and struggles. It's part of stepping into the leadership role. On top of doing coaching with people doing network marketing, I also do consult on the corporate side of network marketing. I was consulting with one company that had hit a couple of their own setbacks, and one of the owners said, "What do I have to do to make my company bulletproof from hardship?" I told him we could get rid of the product, people, and shut the business down. That would really be the only way!

Network marketing is a business that deals with people. People all have different backgrounds, different styles, and different interpretations. When you factor all of that in, you will encounter adversity. Many of my clients have global teams and their adversity comes up dealing with different cultural aspects of business. They need to adjust and adapt to new global markets.

People are going to leave and quit. They may misrepresent you or the company. People are going to gossip about you. This is all part of being part of something like network marketing.

You are going to have setbacks like products running out, the back office not working all the time, and you may even have an owner of your company make a very public mistake. This is all part of the process of being a leader.

Just like we learned from Prada, leaders are the ones that don't get caught up in the drama or focus on the failures. Leaders are the ones that go out and focus on the solution. They are open and curious to figure out what they can do to help or change the trajectory of what happened.

Leaders are the ones that will find a way to parlay every single adversity into a strength, because it is inevitable. You are the captain of the ship, and there are going to be storms when you're out there in the ocean. You've got to learn to steer through the storms and come out the other side. The more impact and influence you have, the more you're going to have adversity.

You can always look for the silver lining. In the collaboration book, Network Marketing Secrets with Top Earners, one of the authors talked specifically about seeing all obstacles as facts. So often we have so many negative thoughts about obstacles that come up. The more we think negatively about them, the more it impacts how we show up. I loved that insight of starting to see obstacles as facts and not something negative that is happening. This is a mark of a true leader.

What can you learn from this? Let me give you an example, and I want you to have your leader hat on to see how you would respond.

Example: a team member leaves and says that they feel the company and/or product doesn't really deliver. What are you thinking? What will you do?

You can argue with them and tell them they are wrong. You can ignore them completely and move on. You can listen to them, thank them for their feedback, and then decide if there is any more action to take.

This is just one example, and you know as a leader that the obstacles in this business will be countless, and I wouldn't ever be able to touch on every single one. But here are some questions I always asked myself on my own team when obstacles came up:

- What can I learn from this?

- Is there anything that I need to do better next time?

- Is there a system that needs to be put in place, tweaked, or followed better?

- Is there a cultural change that needs to be put in place, tweaked, or followed better?

- How is this 100% on me? How can I learn and grow from this?

- Where did their vision stop? How can I nurture vision better next time?

# CHALLENGES ARE YOUR TEST

Challenges can turn into something that is going to help and improve you and your team. There will absolutely be setbacks; it is part of the process. If we can understand it, then we don't have to make it mean anything about us, the company, the industry, or the people involved. Start to look at how you can see your challenges and hardships as a test.

If you can think of an issue you are having right now in network marketing, I have probably faced it when I was in network marketing or one of my coaching clients has. I have always been able to find the silver lining and see it as a test I was taking. But it is because of my dedication to practicing this skill as a leader that I have been able to stop having so much fear and angst about the challenges. Initially when I started out, many times I felt like a victim of the obstacle. I later learned to transition into the survivor and finally into the conqueror. I talk in depth about this process in my book, *The Game on Conquering.*

Your goal as the visionary leader is to be so committed to the industry, your company, and your team that when obstacles come up, you can lead through the obstacle and create a better team from it. So, find a way to take everything that happens, and use it to become a strength, use it as a learning lesson so that you can learn to lead.

Prada and network marketers have some similarities. Just like she said that her work is all consuming, most of us immerse ourselves in the business. The business is us and we are the business. You have done the work, the hustle, the grind. At this phase in leadership, I see people wonder what they are doing. Most people start this business trying to get out of pain. They are barely making ends meet and their pain point is high. If they could make $200 extra a month, the pressure could be released. Once people move out of that, they start to create a lifestyle they want. They start going on trips, buying homes, cars, etc.

But what happens after that? You have gone on all the trips; you are living in the dream house and have several dream cars. At this phase of leadership, I see people start to fizzle out. They have "made it." Leaders have stopped creating vision! It's almost like they think they have graduated from it.

# THE CONTINUOUS VISION

I know we started this book out with vision, but I can't emphasize it enough. You need to continually create a vision for yourself. A visionary leader is not only helping other people with their visions, but they are checking in with themselves, and seeing what part of their vision they have completed and where they need to come up with a bigger vision. You have all heard me say, "New levels, new devils." One of the devils of this phase of leadership is lack of vision again.

As a visionary creator you are in charge of taking something from conception to reality. You have the means to do it too. Think big. One of my clients saw a gap in the training system that her company was using. They didn't ask her to fix it, but she knew that a true leader didn't sit back and say, "Someone else will fix this." She decided to be a visionary leader. She spent months talking to people in the company. She workshopped and took several concepts to other leaders. She had a vision for a new training system and made it happen. This leader truly showed up as a leader. That training system has now replaced the old system in her company. This client decided that her vision was not only to help her own team, but to help her company thrive. She did just that!

What is your NEW vision for the future? Remember the future self-work we did way back in the first few chapters of this book? Well, you are now that future self that you envisioned! How amazing is that?! Once you are now the future version of yourself, your work doesn't stop here. Dream bigger.

I like to call this work the ten thousand-foot view of your life. Often in the daily tasks of our lives, we are in the four-foot view. We are looking at the one or two things we need to do. As a leader in the creation phase, you can effortlessly move from the ten thousand-foot view to the four-foot view. When you look at your life from the ten thousand-foot view, what are you seeing for your future? What is the new vision for your life?

This is often when leaders start to think about their legacy. We are going to talk more in depth about this in chapter 18. But as you work on becoming a leader in this creator phase, I want you to start to think about what that legacy is going to look like. What do you want to be known for?

# LEAD WITH IDEAS NOT EXECUTION

As a leader in this phase, you are also going to be an expert at coming up with ideas and letting others execute them. At one of my seven-figure masterminds, I had someone share that they were exhausted from the business and thinking of retiring. I asked him, "How much time are you spending executing tasks in your business?" He looked at me like I was crazy. "All day," he said. "Who else is supposed to be doing this?" When I told him that he could hire out, automate, and systematize the majority of his business, he was blown away.

He wanted to spend more time mentoring and creating but he couldn't see a way out of the day-to-day of running the business. A visionary leader is dialing in their team at this point. You ask yourself daily, "What am I doing that someone else can do for me?" You may find several things that you keep on that are your main money makers, or maybe your hobby tasks that you like to do but hire out. The rule of thumb is this. If someone else can do it 80% as good as you then you should always outsource. This enables you to double down on your own strengths. It also keeps you from burnout!

People are always shocked to learn how much I hire out in my business. I am not afraid to find people to do things that aren't worth my time. The more time I can invest in being the visionary for my business, the more money I make. One word of caution here. Don't try to hire the one guy that does it all. It never works out for you or him. Hire for the best skills that people offer. Find someone else for everything else.

A visionary leader stays in the vision creation mode as much as they can.

## What you can do right now to work on being a visionary creator:

- Go back and look at the vision that you created in the beginning. See what part of the vision you have achieved.

- Create a new vision for your future. This may include some legacy (more in chapter 18).

- Start to spend more time at the ten thousand-foot view.

- See where you can hire out.

*"The delicate balance of mentoring someone is not creating them in your own image, but giving them the opportunity to create themselves."*

*— Steven Spielberg*

# CHAPTER 15

# THE MENTORING LEADER

Some of my all-time favorite movie characters usually aren't the star of the show. It is the mentors that always intrigue me. Like Mufasa in *Lion King*, Yoda and Obi-Wan in *Star Wars*, or Mr. Miyagi in *Karate Kid*. None of these roles are the main characters, but the story couldn't move forward without them. Each hero needed help so that they could have their triumphant ending. Think about your leaders right now. Each of them is the hero of their own story. That means that you get to decide what role you will play in their story. Stepping into the role of mentor is one of the success milestones that each leader will take.

What makes a truly great mentor? A great mentor has been around the block a few times. They have experienced failure, and they can help others see where obstacles may come up and how to get past them quickly. Great mentors have had their hero's journey and are willing to show others the way. Think back about each mentor that I mentioned from the movies. Every single one has tragedy and triumph in their lives.

One of the hardest parts about leadership is knowing when to lead, when to follow, and when to support. Our intent as leaders is always to help and support our team, but sometimes as we try to help, we become micromanagers. Watching some of my leaders take over after thirty days almost killed me! Just like the movie mentors, I had to realize that it wasn't about me anymore. As a mentor, I wasn't there to swoop in and be the hero. My job was to allow the leader to have their struggle and help them overcome to be the hero of their own story.

It was painful to have them do the presentations when I knew that with my five years of experience, I could do the presentation much better than them. I knew that I had much more credibility to offer. I knew how to close! But what would that have done for the team? I would have missed the opportunity to edify my leaders. I would have skipped out on building their experience and confidence. I would have overlooked the opportunity to know myself when to lead, when to follow, and when to support.

# JUMPING INTO THE MENTORING SPACE

There is a huge difference between mentoring and leading, and it's one of the hardest transitions. In the beginning, you know that you're better than your team. You're better at presenting, you're better at closing, you're better at training.

As your team grows you transition from leader of followers to the leader of leaders. A lot of times people get stuck there, because they are still trying to do everything for their teams. They still are taking too much control rather than mentoring their follower into a leader. People get stuck taking matters into their own hands, and they get stuck in a cycle of having emerging leaders that never emerge! Often people stuck in this leadership phase blame their team, but it may be YOU that is the problem. Here are some common things I hear when leaders are stuck and not transitioning into a mentor role, "I'm doing everything for them." "Why aren't people more motivated?" "It seems like people are willing to show up if I do all the prep work." If these phrases sound familiar to you, you may be stuck in leading and NOT transitioning into mentoring.

I am going to share with you the one tip that will help you transition into your role as a mentor to your emerging leaders. This one tip will change the way you interact with leaders on your team from here on out! If you are transitioning from leader to mentor, do not confuse principles and techniques. This one tip is everything, and bears repeating. Do not confuse principles and techniques!

Someone who is stuck in the leader role needs everything their way. Sometimes they may "allow" someone to do it differently but it's rare. This is called microleading, and it will kill you from creating a legacy business that has leaders upon leaders in your business. Let me give you an example. Let's say you have a business that teaches the technique of third-party validation.

The principle is hearing another voice of third-party validation. The technique that you could think works best is doing a three-way call. Let's say you have another emerging leader that hates doing three-way calls—it's not their style, not their personality—and they have decided they would much rather use group chats and voice messages in group chats for third-party validation. The principle is still the same. The techniques are different.

So as a mentoring promoter you need to pause and ask yourself, "Am I going to be the leader that gets caught up in the technique? OR am I the mentor that is teaching principles focused on empowering this future leader?"

I have watched this play out on many teams. The details may be a bit different, but this theme of leading vs. mentoring is always the same. I can tell you what happens when the seasoned leader doesn't transition into a mentor. A lot of times the emerging leader will resent the seasoned leader. They will start talking back, gossiping, and holding a grudge. They lose respect for their leader, because they aren't willing to step into the role of mentor and let the emerging leader find their own techniques.

Consciously step into the role of mentor. You need to do your best to not confuse principles and techniques and make sure that you're constantly teaching the principle. There may be times when your emerging leader decides to do something different. If the principle is there, get behind them and support them. Ask how to best help them, so that you can continue to raise other leaders among your team.

Becoming a true mentor isn't a title you are just given. In order to be a true mentor, you must possess the 5 C's of mentorship. They are confidence, credibility, competence, candor, and caring. There isn't ONE real mentor out there that doesn't possess all five of these traits. As you move into the role of mentor, ask yourself if you have these five traits when you are mentoring someone. If you are even missing one, you are not truly a mentor yet.

# YOU CAN'T FORCE-FEED SUCCESS

Mentors don't go around forcing people to do things their way. You can't force-feed success to your leaders. Instead of trying to get everybody to see things exactly how you see them, start to understand that everybody sees the world through their own perspective and their own experiences. Success looks different for everyone. Some of your team may be successful on Instagram or Facebook or whichever social media platform you are using. Some are crushing it face to face. Everyone's a little different, and as you become a leader of leaders you must invest in their visions. This is why the 5 C's are so important. When you reach this phase of leadership, it isn't about making people follow you. It's about relying on your skills and expertise and the five C's of mentorship so that people WANT to follow you and want your advice. You are also in a place now that you see that there are several paths to success and not everyone needs to take your path in order to succeed.

The principles are always the same when we're talking about leadership, but the techniques can be a little bit different. Decide for yourself what is the most important way that you can show a specific leader underneath you support. There will be times that they need support, but there will also be times they need to be led, trained, or given feedback. So, whenever you have to categorize things into levels of importance, it will be different for every single person you mentor, but the thing that will stay the same is the 5 C's of mentorship.

Stephen Covey said, "Begin with the end in mind." This is such good advice as you start to develop leaders on your team. I see the struggle that happens with so many people as they start to develop leaders. As new leaders emerge on their team, the leader struggles to know when to be the leader, when to follow, and when to support.

If you begin with the end in mind with your emerging leaders, think about the end game of your network marketing business. Ultimately, we want to be a leader of the biggest and best leaders in the industry. We want people that are empowered and not needing us every step of the way. We want leaders that are examples in the company of thinking innovatively and duplicating our system of creating more leaders.

# FEEDBACK VS. HANG BACK

You need to learn when to give feedback, and when to hang back. This means check in as your developing leaders start to do their own thing. One question I love to ask myself is, "Is what they are doing going to harm the team?" If not, it may be a chance to see what they can come up with. The worst thing that can happen is that you let them go and gain some experience. You know you have a system, feedback, or coaching that you can give to them if they try something, and it fails. BUT, the experience and encouragement that you give the developing leader will be priceless.

The key to this type of leadership is good communication. Make sure to be honest, let them know your intention, and remind yourself that you are giving opinions, not hard rules. One big failure that leaders make is not continuously working on their communication skills. As a leader who is working with emerging leaders, you must be investing in your own communication skills. I see very bad communicators and it stalls their business.

One person that attended one of my masterminds was talking about how her team kept telling her she was coming off offensive. She said, "If that is what they think, that's their problem. I am just very bold." Bold and blind to feedback is a deadly combination! This leader had people giving her feedback and she wasn't listening. I am not telling you that you have to change completely, but you have to be willing to work on your communication. How can you convey what you want to get across in a way that will help others be more receptive? This was one of the skills that you learned early on in this book, but I wanted to bring it up again in the Legacy phase of leadership. You are never too great to get feedback. Remember that. Feedback should always be coming in. Now, who you listen to is another story, but you should always be willing to hear it and decide what to do with it.

Let's put this back on our example of being a leader of leaders. If the woman above was one of your emerging leaders, what would you do? At times, you've got to step in. You've got to lead at times when your organization or emerging leader is struggling. The woman above was at my mastermind because she had five great potential leaders quit her team in the past. She wasn't able to keep leaders around because she was "bold." As a leader of leaders, you have to know what investment is going to make the most impact for your team.

Here's another example that I want you to think about as a leader of leaders. You have a leader on your team that has stopped sponsoring. They have solid leaders, and so they have started to get into management mode. They are telling their team what to do but aren't doing any of the actions themselves. What do you do as that leader's leader? I love the saying: "The speed of the leader, the speed of the pack." We know that whatever we do well duplicates sometimes. Whatever we do poorly duplicates almost always.

I see this with my kids. If you are a parent, you know exactly what I'm talking about. My kids do whatever I do poorly. I swear almost all of them follow and do the things I do poorly. Whatever I do amazing duplicates with some of my kids, some of the time. It's the same thing in business.

Great leaders are always learning principles from other leaders. They learn how they're going to apply the techniques with their own style, authenticity, boldness, and with their own personality. You should always be looking and assessing as a leader to see what your team needs. You've got to also learn when to follow, and when to empower. We are going to talk about how important recognition is in the following chapters. As a leader you need to know what inspires, motivates, comforts, and encourages other people.

# ALLOW SOME FAILURE ALONG THE WAY

One of the most empowering tools I found when I was building network marketing was allowing my leaders to fail. This may sound crazy to some of you. But remember the goal is to create leaders that I don't have to micromanage. I was going to teach them, talk to them and help them. But I was also going to let them go out and try and fail. Failure is the best feedback that we can support our team through.

If you have a kid that's learning how to walk, you don't go and grab them every time they wobble. You don't stop them from falling or even trying to walk. You're going to try to help them, maybe get the little broom out so they hold onto it as they walk. After a couple of steps this way you are going to put the broom away and watch what happens. There will be more falls, but you are there supporting, not doing it for them.

In my organization, I was always working through the balance of when to lead, when to follow and when to support—especially as a leader of leaders. My goal was to support. I would always lead by giving my thoughts and vision, but if they were doing something completely different it wasn't a problem. My leaders already knew what my thoughts were and if they went a different direction, I would tell them my job was to support them.

I remember one leader wanted to do things quite differently than I did. At first, I wanted to tell him no and argue why my way was better, but then I remembered my main goal was to support. I said, "Look, I'm here to support you. So, if this is how you want to do it, let's do it! If there is any way I can help you I am here." It changed the dynamic of how we worked together through that project.

We sat down and he explained his thought process and I adjusted my feedback to fit into what he was wanting to accomplish. I told him as long as he wasn't doing something that would lead the team astray, I was there to support him.

Your leaders are entrepreneurs. Don't make anyone feel like there is only one way to do it. That doesn't help emerging leaders learn. Allow them to fail forward, and you will see them have success.

Another great tip I love to give as you lead emerging leaders. Ask them if it's okay to give them feedback throughout. Be part of their team of support. I found that as I did this with my own leaders, they sometimes came up with brilliant projects that we would then go and implement with the whole team. Some didn't work and it failed, but it was ok. It was feedback for that leader to go and try something else. Build the relationship with your leaders where they know that you will be leading, following, and supporting them the whole way. It is such a great dynamic to learn at this process of leadership.

# BRANDING REFRESH

At this phase of leadership, you should have a very established brand. This is why people like you, buy with you, and build a business with your help. Your brand is how you show up in your business and why people do business with you. As you transition into the legacy phase of leadership, you will want to look at a rebrand. I am not saying you should completely drop your brand, but you want to look at refreshing it. This rebrand is all about incorporating more of you and what you stand for. As you become a legacy leader, you will be focusing more on your commitment to causes, serving, and the community. It is essential that you start infusing this in your brand if you haven't already done it.

Although many top earners and leaders have not created a brand it is one big step that will create massive leverage for you. A brand isn't what you think about yourself, it is what the world thinks about you. Part of creating a next-level brand is to first master one platform and become an authority figure on that platform. Next is to repurpose content to multiple platforms. For example, I create one video and from that video, my team repurposes that same content into a podcast, blog post, written post, Instagram post and YouTube Video. Not every piece of content works out where you can repurpose and not every top leader follows this strategy, but it is definitely one that works. If attention is the #1 currency of marketing, then why wouldn't you create content and put it out everywhere? If you are newer, this strategy wouldn't work at all. If you are in the learner phase you will find one platform and focus on it but keep this strategy in mind as you break through to new levels in your business.

This is also a time that you are going to be more well known for being a successful businessperson and not just the highest ranked person in your company. One of my leaders was shocked when she got asked to speak at a "women in business" conference. She was terrified to speak to a group of people outside of network marketing. She was very confident inside of network marketing, but she hadn't worked on branding herself outside of the industry. Part of being a legacy leader can be stepping into leadership and your personal brand outside of network marketing. Each leader is going to find the path which suits them the best but when you are growing a large business you always want to think in terms of leverage. Branding done right is LEVERAGE.

As you think about your brand "refresh" here are a couple of things to consider:

- How do you use your mission, vision, and values in your brand?

- How do you want people outside the industry to see you?

- What are you known for in and out of your business?

- What can your message be to the general population? How is your brand an example of that?

- How do you fit your legacy into your personal brand?

This is a hot topic I will be presenting and speaking more about at my next mastermind event. As a mentoring leader, we are always reminding ourselves where leaders are and training them on what skills they need to learn. The brand refresh is a great way to train your leaders on how they can create a personal brand for themselves.

## What you can do right now to work on being a mentoring leader:

- Know the difference between a mentor and a leader.

- Start to define the role of mentor to your leaders and teams.

- Work on releasing the control. Promote the growth of others by asking them to show up before they may be 100% ready.

- Remember that even though you know that you can most likely do things better than many of your team members, you must be willing to FOSTER THEM on their hero journey.

- Start to create a plan for yourself and emerging leaders for how to create a brand and culture.

*"Teamwork is the ability to work together towards a common vision. The ability to direct individual accomplishment toward organizational objectives. It is the fuel that allows common people to attain uncommon results."*

*— Andrew Carnegie*

# CHAPTER 16

# THE LEGACY
# LEADER

Whenever I think of the ultimate tribe creator and coach, I think of Jesus Christ. Whether you are a follower, believer, or naysayer of Jesus, His life is a great example. Jesus had a skill of creating followers out of unbelievers, and He followed a pattern. I daresay Jesus would be the ultimate network marketer!

As Jesus was teaching the people, He did four things that helped Him build His followers from a handful to thousands. First, He prepared. Just like we have covered in previous chapters, Jesus prepared Himself. He spent time preparing Himself through learning, obeying God's commandments, and applying His own teaching into His life.

Second, Jesus invited people to come and listen. He gave everyone a compelling reason to come and listen to His teachings. For some it was the invitation to repent, for others it was an invitation to be healed. He gave every individual person an invitation to come.

Third, He asked them to follow. He asked them to come and try what He was teaching them about. Jesus invited people to come and spend time with Him and see what He was up to. People weren't being told what to do, they were simply being shown how Jesus lived His life and then invited to do the same.

Finally, Jesus encouraged people to grow. He invited them to believe something they may have never believed before. He spoke to His followers about putting themselves out there for what they now believed in. He offered encouragement to come closer to God.

These four steps helped Jesus create followers, or what we now call a tribe. He created people that were all in with what He was saying. Tribes or followers are so important as we grow into this next version of a leader.

# THE OPPORTUNITY AND RESPONSIBILITY OF LEADERSHIP

At this point, you will have people in your team, and you may even be creating a successful team that has emerging leaders underneath you. But I wanted to speak specifically to creating tribes is the part of your leadership journey for a specific reason.

You have the experience, expertise, and knowledge just like Jesus did. Jesus had the opportunity to do many things with this version of Himself. He was tried and tested many times. He could have decided to say and do whatever He wanted with His tribe of followers.

You have that same opportunity and responsibility. As a leader, you have people that are looking up to you. They look to you to see what sort of a person you are both in and out of your business. When you think about leading a tribe, I want you to think about what sort of impact you are leaving on the tribe.

I heard stories of a leader partying hard with alcohol and women while he was at a generic networking event. He thought it wouldn't be a big deal. No one from his team was there, and he had left the wife and kids at home. He just needed to blow off some stress for a weekend. What he didn't realize was that one weekend cost him his marriage, his family, and eventually his entire network marketing team.

This man had built his team around family values, and it was a driving factor of why people signed up to join him. When word (and pictures) got out of his partying ways that weekend people started to see that he wasn't the same man in public as he was in private. His decisions that weekend caused a catastrophic turn in his life. As you become the leader to leaders, be willing to stand for what you feel is right at all times and in all places. This is part of leadership. You have to talk the talk and walk the walk everywhere you go. I was once staying at a resort with my family. We were having adventures every day and always playing by the pool as a family. One day while I was at the pool a woman approached me and said that she follows me on social media and had a network marketing business. She told me it was so great to see that my "real" life matched my "social" life.

# THE CULTURE OF LEADING

We have already covered in previous chapters how vital creating culture is. Culture is one of the most important aspects of becoming a better leader at this phase of your business. Sure, you may have created culture, but how are you continually checking on it, adjusting it, and cultivating the culture you want to lead? In the legacy phase of leadership, the number of members you have on your team are all going to contribute to the type of culture you create. You cannot create a culture that you are not willing to live by. You will eventually be found out, and it will crush your business. No, this doesn't mean you won't make mistakes, but be who you are. Be proud of who you are. Create a culture around who you are. If I was posting pictures about loving to vacation with my family, and then in real life I was doing something different, everyone would find out. That woman didn't come and talk to me the first day she recognized me. (She told me this.) She recognized me, and then anytime she saw us she was taking note if I was doing what I said I do. This is culture. Tribes follow people because they believe that person is the person they say they are.

I have said this before, but you must CONSCIOUSLY build culture and tribes, OR they will build themselves. Remember the difference between naturally building and authentically building that we talked about previously. The natural culture will always build itself, but it may not be authentic to what you are wanting to create and cultivate. Whenever you get a group of people together, they naturally start to build a type of culture and certain tribe around the events, people there, etc. At this level of leadership, you need to be consciously creating and always adjusting to the authentic culture you are wanting to be a part of.

Here's the crazy thing about becoming a leader that consciously creates tribes, and why I wanted to discuss it again in this phase of leadership. Tribe and team culture are always changing. Some people see this as a challenge because it is always evolving and growing. I like to think of it as a good thing because YOU are always evolving and changing. Think back to what you thought you wanted your team to be in the beginning vs. what it is now. It has changed, and hopefully for the better. But like I said before, it doesn't matter if you have one team member or one hundred thousand; your team culture will create itself, or you can consciously create a solid culture for your team.

At this phase of leadership, you are also working on juggling the culture of other leaders and what they have set up for their own individual teams. Maybe they are starting to have their own team parties, groups, etc. How you lead as a legacy leader is going to really show up as you start to navigate the waters of having your own culture and supporting the culture of your top leaders.

# THE CULTURE SUPPORTS THE GOALS

This year I have had the awesome opportunity to be a tennis coach for my kids' high school tennis team. It is incredible to watch my own children grow in a game I am so passionate about, but it is also incredible to watch other kids grow in their ability and talents on and off the court. As soon as I said yes to coaching these teams, I knew one huge responsibility I was taking on was creating a culture with the teams. One of the biggest parts of this is making every single person feel important. That means loving them where they are at. I know on any team there are going to be huge superstars and people that are excited they made it. Some of these kids' victory was getting on the varsity team. Others were excited to make it on JV. Part of leading with legacy is SEEING people and what they want. Then you take it to the next level and find unique ways to include them and support them in their goals.

The business behind that business is creating that culture off the court as well. In tennis practice, we focus a lot on their skills sets, mentality, etc. But then we also create spaces for the team to bond, grow, socialize, and make it fun. We create trips for the team so that they will intentionally be able to create their space in the tribe. We also do dinners like the end of the year banquet, and we do a varsity dinner right before they go to state so that they can really focus on being part of the community.

A lot of creating the culture is small things like creating a group chat. Every week I will send something that has nothing to do with tennis. I want them to feel excited and feel like they are a part of something. It is the law of likeability.

Marry the process and date the results. Every little detail matters when you are a legacy leader. You should be intentionally loving people where they are at while helping people envision a future that they can have and how to get there. Part of this is getting buy-in! People want to feel like they get to collaborate with you and that they have a say in what is happening. Prior to coaching my kids' teams, I was coaching another team for fourteen years. Eleven of those fourteen years the team took state. This year I have loved to create the blueprint all over again and watch it go to work. This year the girl's tennis team did it. They took state! That had nothing to do with me. It had everything to do with these girls following the blueprint and being all in. My job as a legacy leader/coach of the team was to facilitate that. As you look at your team, I want you to ask yourself, "How am I facilitating growth? How am I mentoring and coaching my leaders? How am I stepping out of the way and letting them create their own success?"

In network marketing, one of the excuses I hear is, "I don't have a huge team." Doesn't matter. Start small. If you don't have a huge team, as Stephen Covey says, you need to "begin with the end in mind." There are so many things you can do to create a tribe in network marketing.

# THEY WANT THE CULTURE YOU ARE OFFERING

The first thing you need to do is understand that the vast majority of people inside of network marketing are actually paying to be part of a community. Yes, you read that correctly. People are paying to be part of a community. Many of you may be shaking your heads thinking, "That doesn't make sense." People pay to be part of a community all the time. There are thousands of different communities that people pay to be in.

People pay to be in the culture and community at various places. We talked about this before. One of the areas that people pay to be a part of is at the gym. My wife has a gym community that she has been part of for years. She loves the women, loves the activity, and has met some of her closest friends there. She pays to be part of that culture. We all have communities that we are paying to be a part of because we want to be part of that culture.

The same thing goes in network marketing. There are people that are absolutely here for the culture and community. They want to be part of a tribe. We all have different kinds of tribes—maybe it's a sports team, maybe it's a specific talent or hobby that you have, but we all have that need for a sense of belonging.

In network marketing, this is truly the business behind the business. If you want to create a next-level type of business, you really need to challenge yourself to intentionally creating your culture. You have to ask yourself questions about what your community is going to look like, what your culture will be. I promise you if you don't go and intentionally create a culture for your team, it will create one for itself, and you may not like what it looks like. One woman that came to me for coaching told me that her team had got a reputation for partying too hard at conventions. She said she never wanted that type of reputation associated with her team. When I asked her what type of culture she did want she said, "Anything but that!" She hadn't clearly defined what the culture of the team was, and so it naturally became something that she didn't want. You have to be in charge of creating culture and checking in on it. Be willing to adjust and adapt when your team gets bigger, and you start to have more of your own leaders on your team.

In my very first book *The Game of Networking*, I talked about the importance of culture. One of the things I did when I was working in a network marketing company is we created a day called R.A.K.. It stood for random acts of kindness day. We had a random act of kindness blitz day, and we would encourage our team to do as many random acts of kindness as they could. I was blown away by what a ripple effect this created for our team. We had people doing everything from calling or texting people and telling them how much they meant to them to people paying for random strangers' gas. People donated their time, talents, money, and possessions to others. One man even went and helped a neighbor out with roofing his house. They had lived by each other for a decade and never met one another. This man on my team drove by and saw his neighbor and son up on the roof and walked over with a nail gun in hand. It created a neighborly friendship that wouldn't have happened if it weren't for the R.A.K. day.

This was completely done intentionally on my part. I wanted to create a culture of service on my team. I knew that being able to create days like this would promote service and be something that would spread on our team. This created the type of culture and feel inside the team, and it also created a fun factor that I am always wanting to incorporate into team culture.

You want to make people feel good about themselves for being part of the culture you have created. I've seen teams get together and do extremely fun things whether it's online or offline. Teams show up to their conventions and they are known for being part of the team. Their leader has intentionally created a culture that others want to be a part of. I was up shopping in downtown Salt Lake City with my wife and there was a network marketing event. I noticed a group of women in matching shirts and bags walk by laughing and enjoying themselves. Another group of women that were not with their group commented, "I wish we did fun things like that as a team." People want to be part of a culture and community that they are proud of.

Creating culture doesn't mean that you have to buy shirts or bags. Culture is all about creating qualities and attributes that you want your team to be known for. It can be things that are done completely for free. You can think of things you can do inside of your Facebook group that could be fun or funny or goofy. Everybody could dress up on a Zoom call and when it's during the holiday season, you could have an ugly sweater Zoom call. There are so many different ideas that you could do. But you must do it intentionally and build around the type of culture you want to create.

# RECOGNITION GOES A LONG WAY . . . EVEN FOR YOUR TOP LEADERS

Part of creating culture is recognition. As mentioned earlier, men die for it, women cry for it. I've seen many teams that think they're very good at recognition and they get stagnant doing the same thing over and over again. They stop thinking of new ideas. Recognition needs to be something that is evolving and changing along with your culture. I would challenge you to think of how many different ways you can recognize your team based on the culture of recognition. It, of course, can be based on results as well, but you want to think of as many ways as you can to recognize the most people. This could be a shout-out to the person with the best results for the week. It could be the results for the month. It could be when someone starts and gets their very first sign up or when someone makes their first post or when someone joins the team or when it's someone's birthday. You could do recognition as well. Spotlight of the week of somebody that's on the team. In my first collaboration book, *Recruit Your Way to Six Figures*, one of the authors shared about a contest called "Go for No" that she does with her team.

She celebrates people going out and getting the most no's to different things like product, business opportunity, hosting a party, etc. It is so brilliant. She is recognizing effort put in, not just numbers. As a result, she has watched her numbers increase dramatically.

Remember men die for it, women cry for recognition. The number one reason why people leave jobs is lack of appreciation, it is not income. Recognition is critical in creating the culture of your business. You must understand the importance and value of creating culture, and then go out and create a plan around it.

Create a team theme. Figure out what your cause is. Make up a team motto. Know what you are all about and create something that's bigger than in your business. In chapter 18 we are going to dive into creating a legacy and a movement that is at the next level in your community and tribe of network marketing. But you have to start here with your culture first.

# IT'S NOT ABOUT WHO YOU ARE, BUT HOW YOU TREAT PEOPLE

I got to introduce a very well-known person at an event. This person had created a whole tribe around values and qualities that they said they personally lived. I was excited to introduce them, and it just so happened that this person was someone my wife loved too. I invited my wife backstage before the presentation to meet with the person. It turned out the person was not who they showed themselves to be. They ended up being the complete opposite of who my wife and I thought they were. I am not going to go into details about what we encountered, but let me just say if there was an award for "influencer acting award" this person would have won it. They were completely different in person than they were online. After that backstage interaction, both my wife and I stopped following the person and didn't buy any of their products anymore. It felt like the tribe they had built was built on a complete lie. This person created a fictional character so they would sell the most product. No one likes to be duped! Be your authentic self as you grow into a huge business with thousands of people on your team.

Another person I knew in network marketing was famous for her warm personality on her training and lives on Facebook. People on her team always said that they felt like her best friend even though they hadn't met her in person. So, you can imagine people's excitement to meet her at a team event. This woman did not present the same way at the event as she did online. She actually had paid bouncers to keep people away from her! She called me after one particular company event. She had shown up with her bouncers and would not engage with any one of her team that she didn't have a scheduled meeting with. When she called me, she said she had a "mass exodus" of members from her team after the event. Her team had felt hurt that she wouldn't talk with them, other leaders in the company were disgusted with how she showed up, and she was completely mortified by what was being said about her after the event.

As a leader creating a tribe, you need to be the same person wherever you are found. Whether it be online, in person, at an event or a small gathering. Now, this doesn't mean you can't create boundaries. You absolutely have to have boundaries, but always remember where your success has come from. You couldn't have a business without customers, builders, and YOUR raving fans.

In this phase of leadership, you are really working on becoming a legacy. Maybe that sounds bold or stuck up, but it is true. Think back on history. Who are the people that are remembered? Who are the people that their stories live on long after they are gone? They are the legacy leaders that used their talents to build something unique and special.

One of the most inspiring things about our business is the amount of impact that each of us can have in the Legacy phase of leadership. I believe that the good of this world is being funded, guided, and led by leaders from network marketing. Every single place I go, I look AND find evidence that this is true. In order to make the biggest impact in the world, we all need to step into leading as a legacy leader. We need to stop shying away from it or thinking that it is stuck up. We do the most good when we lead from legacy and then show others how to do it. Please, hear me out. Becoming a legacy leader is going to make some people uncomfortable. You may even find that your inner circles of friends change as you work on yourself and step into legacy leadership. That's ok. We need you. The very best version of you. We need you to lead from legacy. We need you to see the vision of YOUR story lasting centuries and being inspirational for generations. Don't shy away from legacy leadership because of your limiting beliefs. OWN it and create a legacy worth talking about.

## What you can do right now to work on being a legacy leader:

- Take leadership seriously and always be preparing with setting systems and culture strategies in place to create a team others would want to be on.

- Be always inviting people to join and using social strategies to brand your team and themselves.

- Know that people are looking to you to be the example.

- Set and live by standards everywhere you go that you want to be known for.

- Step into legacy leadership and write down the story that you want to be told about yourself.

*"Bosses push, leaders pull. Real leadership is servant leadership."*

*– Dave Ramsey*

# CHAPTER 17

# THE SERVANT LEADER

A young man was getting ready to enter the military. He had been dreaming of being a soldier since he was small. When he was twelve, he learned how to shoot a gun. In high school, he would go running every single day in preparation for boot camp. He spent dedicated time learning from books, documentaries, and YouTube about how to be a great soldier.

The day he left for boot camp, this young man's dad came to him and said, "I know how much you are looking forward to this. It is going to be much different than you think it is. But, that's ok. I know you will get through this." The young man laughed a little. He knew his dad would always see him as a kid. His dad didn't understand how prepared he was to go. The dad went on, "I want you to do one thing for me, son. Promise me that every single day you will pick a different person in your group to serve. It doesn't matter if you fill his water bottle up for him, shine his shoes, or make his bed. You serve one person every single day in your group." The son wasn't expecting this request, but he promised his dad he would, and he left for boot camp.

All through boot camp, the son kept that promise to his dad. He found someone every single day to serve. When boot camp came to an end, the son had made service a habit and he kept serving someone daily throughout his entire military career. Every single day he found someone to serve. Years later when this young man had become a decorated soldier and leader in the military, he was sitting with his dad talking about the day he entered boot camp. The son asked his dad, "That day I left for boot camp, why did you make me promise to serve every single day?"

The dad said, "I knew you were destined for greatness. I knew you were going to be a great soldier. But, you had the arrogance and self-importance of a teenager. Leaders serve other people and that was a skill you hadn't worked on yet. I wanted you to learn how to serve others so that you would be able to become a great leader in the military and NOT just a great soldier. I knew you could be both."

# SERVICE IS ULTIMATE LEADERSHIP

For two years I dedicated my entire life to serving others. I spent two years serving the people every single day while on a mission for my church. I learned so much while I spent two whole years in service. One of the main things I learned is how serving others intently creates an instant love for them. If you ever find yourself struggling with a person on your team, or a particular leader on your team has become difficult, serve them. Servant leadership shows that you are willing to put aside differences, be the bigger person, and helps to remind us that everyone needs help.

As a leader in this phase, you are past making it about yourself. You know that you make the most money as you step into mentoring, leading, and serving your team. Let me be completely honest with you. Anyone can create personal success. I truly believe this. When we are trying to create wealth, success, and dial in focus it is easy to show up for ourselves. But stepping into the creator level of leadership means that you are stepping into a whole new way of thinking. You are now MORE focused on creating and supporting other people's success than just your own.

I see people "retire" at this stage of their business because they feel like they have done it all. They have created wealth and success. They have leveled up their lifestyle and all their wildest dreams have come true. They get bored, burnt out, and distracted. Here's the thing. This person is still only focused on themselves. They haven't shifted the focus to the thousands of other people that they can help. Now, don't get me wrong, you can absolutely retire whenever you want to! But let it be for the right reasons and not because you are feeling this way. This is why this phase of leadership is so important for people that are making this amount of money and have been in network marketing for this long. You have got to move into becoming the CREATOR and shift into servant leadership.

In tennis, I loved competing by myself. I knew that if I won or lost, that was on me. When I played doubles, I had to be just as concerned about my partner as I was about myself. My focus couldn't always be on me. I had to be anxiously engaged in my partner's mental state, practice regime, and performance. His success was my success. When I figured this out, it became a passion of mine to figure out how I could serve my tennis partner. I would go out of my way to make sure that I brought the drink and snacks he liked. I would encourage him to get a good night's sleep and offer him some positive self-talk that he could use during our matches. His personal success was my success.

I was watching a tennis match once and one partner's shoelaces broke. They called for a break, and I heard the guy with the broken lace say, "What am I supposed to do?" His partner was already pulling something out of his own bag. He had brought an extra pair of shoelaces that he let his partner use. I thought that was a great example of being anxiously engaged in another person. But this leader didn't stop there. I was blown away when this guy let his partner rest while he laced up his shoes for him. He even put them on his feet and tied them tight! This was complete servant leadership in action. Servant leaders are anxiously engaged in the care and welfare of others. They are willing to show up better than sometimes people show up for themselves. Ask yourself, "What does servant leadership look like in my business? How am I anxiously engaged with others and helping them have success?"

# TAKE CARE OF YOURSELF BY HIRING HELP

It can become almost impossible to step into this phase of leadership if you aren't taking care of yourself. I want you to look at your own personal daily methods of operation. How are you taking care of yourself mentally, physically, emotionally, spiritually, and financially? At this phase, you can afford to hire help and assistance. Do it! Don't wait until you have burnt yourself out and are desperate. Hire help as quickly as you can so that you can stay on top of your game and can take optimal care of yourself. One of the leading causes of burnout in this phase is not treating your six- and seven-figure business like a successful business.

Could you imagine the CEO of a corporate company cleaning the toilets of the building? Probably wouldn't happen. That is because the CEO is getting paid to do their job to the best of their ability. I want anyone in this phase of leadership to ask yourself, "What is my job?" Make a list of things that are actually your job. Next, make a list of all the things you are doing right now. Put everything down. Now, take both lists and compare. Anything that is not "your job" you will need to hire out and find someone to do it for you.

A big mindset block for people stepping into this phase of leadership is worrying about what people will think of them if they start to hire out different tasks in their business and their home. They worry that their team will think they don't want to communicate with them if they hire a virtual assistant to answer or an email. They worry that their neighbor will judge them if they get a nanny or have a lawn maintenance crew come and take care of their yard. Here is a simple solution—stop worrying about what other people think. At this phase of network marketing, we should be used to the judgments of others! But like I mentioned before, "new levels, new devils." Don't be surprised if you have the fear of judgment coming up again in this level of leadership. It happens, and you need to plan for it, and not be surprised when you see it pop up. Acknowledge it, see what's coming up for you, and then ask yourself, "How much time could I gain by having someone else do this for me?" That question always makes it a no-brainer for me to hire help.

Once I have convinced people that they need to hire help, the next question I get is, "Where can I start looking?" I wish there was a cut-and-dried answer for this, but there are countless places to look. Here are a couple of things to consider as you go to hire help. First, do I have a mission, vision, or values around who I want to help? An example of this is my client that was dedicated to helping single moms in her area. If you do, this will help you narrow down your search. Second, look at your own network and connections. Is there anyone that you can ask for recommendations? Usually, you will have several people that have been hired for the type of help you are looking for and they can be a great resource. That is one of the great perks to being in the Leader of Leaders Mastermind groups. The members of this group are amazing at sharing resources and helping one another out. One member was in total panic over having to hire a new nanny. She didn't know what to do or where to start looking. Another member had just gone through this at the beginning of the year, and they sat at dinner one night and talked all about how to find the best nanny online, what to look for, and how much to pay. That is networking done right! Third, use your online network. People are so willing to help when you are looking for something. Use social media to your advantage and post something about needing help. You will be shocked at who you connect with. I have done this several times with projects I have needed help with. I have several team members that I got this way and we have been working together for years.

# THE STATUS QUO IS FOR THE AVERAGE JOE

We all create the status quo in our minds of where we want to be. Most of the time, we hit them. But at this phase, you should be moving past them in these areas of your life. Let's look at your physical life for example. It doesn't matter if you work out five days a week or once a month. I want you to think about how you are going to crank it up a notch and push yourself. You may be wondering why this matters at this phase of leadership, or WHY it matters at all in leadership.

People want to follow people that are inspiring. Status quo usually doesn't inspire. I like to say that the status quo is for the average Joe. You all know the guy. The guy that is fine living paycheck to paycheck. The guy that thinks that personal development is weak. The guy that drowns his fears in booze and over-consuming. The status quo has never created leadership energy that helps motivate and inspire others. See where you are just living in the status quo. If you are super active, people are USED to you being active. They may have seen your daily 20-mile bike rides as inspiring at first, but the newness wears down and it becomes the status quo. Where do you want to improve? Where do you want to inspire? You must be willing to push yourself, and that does create pressure. There is pressure to continue to push past normal. There is pressure to be an example. But at this phase of leadership, legacy leaders thrive under the pressure. They know how to manage it and create from it. They understand and welcome the pressure to be an example and serve others.

Let me explain one of the obstacles that I see at this phase of leadership. At this legacy phase of leadership you are pretty far removed from a lot of struggles and hardships that your newest person is going through. I'm not saying you don't have struggles, but they often look different than other people's. As some people say, at this phase of leadership we are dealing with "first world problems." We may have struggled in the beginning like our newest people, but often that hasn't been your struggle for quite some time. When we can always be pushing and growing intentionally in our lives, we stay connected to the struggle, failure, and disappointment. Sure, the struggle isn't the same, but we know what it feels like. Servant leaders don't have to struggle, but they hold themselves to the standard of always reaching for the next hard thing to always be in the cycle of growth.

In this phase, you have to take ultimate accountability for yourself and your life, and you also help others do the same. You now need to be the ultimate example to others to show them the way. You can't have huge gaps and be suffering through big things and serve others. If you cut off an arm, it's hard to serve someone else while you are bleeding out. I watch people do this over and over again and fail. They reach this level of success, and then forget that they are the example to others! People are looking to you as an example, what are they seeing?

Now, you probably will never cut an arm off, but ask yourself if you are cut off mentally, physically, spiritually, or emotionally. If you are, I am going to tell you again . . . get help! You may see a theme emerging in this book. Leaders ask for help. Leaders pay for help. Leaders are invested in living their best lives. We serve the best when our own personal needs are met. As a leader in this phase, you can afford every single help that is offered to you. You get to decide what type of help to get but invest in help so that you can turn around and serve those people on your team that need you.

# GET YOUR HOUSE IN ORDER

Servant leadership starts with you. It then moves into focusing on others and what they need. If you have yourself in order, it becomes easy to take care of yourself. Let's take something that most Americans can relate to. In 2020 during the pandemic, there was a rush on toilet paper. Who knew it would become the hot commodity of 2020?! I watched in astonishment as people rushed every single store, and every single online venue to grab toilet paper. I was talking to a friend about it, and she said, "Someone I look up to has been telling us for years to get our houses in order and that included having a year's supply of everything, including toilet paper. I have been working on getting it bit by bit for years, and so this toilet paper shortage doesn't really impact our family at all. BUT, being prepared means that we have the means to help other people who aren't so lucky."

This woman became the toilet paper service for her neighbors that weren't as prepared for the next few weeks until toilet paper became available again. She was able to be in servant leadership because she had her own house in order. I asked her if she ever worried that she would run out and then not have any for her own family. She said, "I'm smart. If that happens, I will figure it out! There are people all over the world that don't even use toilet paper!" Funny example, but this illustrates ultimate servant leadership. This woman would NOT be able to even think about serving if she hadn't been preparing for years. It is impossible to serve others when our own lives are in dire need. You have got to take care of yourself first and then you are ready to help others!

The other thing that stood out to me is that this woman wasn't serving from fear. She didn't say, "You can have one roll but that's it!" She posted in her neighborhood Facebook group telling the entire neighborhood that she had supplies and was willing to share. People came and she never once turned anyone away. Servant leadership never happens from fear. If you are fearful of serving certain leaders on your team because they may outrank you, you are not in servant leadership. Servant leaders are never fearful of serving their team and community.

A note here about servant leadership. I have seen people be really focused and prepared in their physical life and starving in their spiritual life. They can offer servant leader energy in their physical life BUT not in the spiritual. This is why it is important to get your whole "house" in order. Do a mental checklist or even take a couple of minutes right now to see where you are ready to step into servant leadership, and where you may need to spend some more time really getting yourself and that area of your life in order. I remember when I did a mental check of my "whole house" several years ago. I felt very confident in some areas, but there were a couple that I knew I was neglecting. As I thought about those areas of my life, I could clearly see two paths presenting themselves to me. I could be overwhelmed, ashamed, and continue to neglect those areas, OR I could take accountability, see where I was at, and create a game plan to increase in those areas. Of course, I chose the latter one. I am so grateful I did. I now look at getting my house in order and see that those areas that I focused on have improved.

One of my coaching clients talked to me about having huge success in her business. But while she was doing that, she had let her spiritual self-start fade. She said she didn't feel balanced and that it was hard sometimes to not feel hollow. How many of you can relate? She set up a plan to start pouring into herself spiritually and it made a huge difference not only for her, but even for her team. Find the weakness in yourself and strengthen it!

# HEALTHY AND UNHEALTHY EGO

Now let's talk about one of the major obstacles for servant leaders. EGO. Ego goes right into getting your house in order. Ego is all about "your inner house." I can already hear some of you say right now, "But Rob, having an ego is what got me to where I am today. Every successful person has an ego!" I agree! But at this phase of leadership, we have got to learn how to dim the ego in order to serve. We need to learn the difference between a healthy ego and an unhealthy ego. Servant leaders are willing to set aside differences, struggles, and their own ego to serve others. Think about it this way, there are light switches that you can flip on and off. There are also light switches that have a dimmer setting on them. You can slowly turn the light higher and lower. In the creator phase of leadership, your ego should be on a dimmer that is on demand. You should be able to dim it at any time.

When your ego gets too high, you start to focus on yourself. You think only about how it will impact you. You won't show up and serve unless it has a direct impact on you. I watched someone tank their team. Every time this person's leaders would come and ask for help or even mentorship, this person would ask, "What are you going to do for me?" They were too ME-focused! They hadn't learned how to dim the ego. I promise you that servant leadership will come back tenfold. It may not be direct, but I have seen it time and again that the people that lead from servant leadership are taken care of in ways they couldn't imagine.

One of my client's companies came to them and asked them to help get a training model together for the whole company. He helped without hesitating. When other leaders asked him how much he was getting paid, he said, "I don't know yet, but they always take care of me." The other people called him foolish. He started to question himself and if he should demand the company pay him. After we spoke, he decided it felt best for him to stay in servant leadership to his company and see this as a labor of love that he was happy to do for them. The training launched and was a HUGE success. The company did something I have never seen any other company do for this guy. It was a huge bonus that was completely unexpected. He was also put onto a council that now puts him in the room where all the big decisions for the company are made. This guy didn't know any of this was on the other end of his serving. He worked from servant leadership and was happy to help. Tenfold it came back to him! This example isn't going to work for everyone, but I wanted to share it because it is a great example of this man taking servant leadership to heart. When other people started to have opinions about what was going on, he had to really look into himself for the answer to what was right. He couldn't ask other people or look it up online. He had to decide for himself what felt right and be completely at peace with whatever the outcome was.

This phase of leadership is a challenge to duplicate and create a system around because so much of this comes from your innermost self. Servant leadership is driven by your deepest desire and beliefs about you. As much as I can share the blueprint for the level of leadership, you will never get the exact map until you include the directions that you know about yourself here. Many of you have heard me talk about the public, personal, and private versions of ourselves. Servant leaders have a clear vision of the private version of themselves and that is where they are leading from.

# KNOW WHEN TO HOLD 'EM

Servant leaders put aside differences. I have NEVER, not once, seen anyone make it to this level of leadership and not had differences come up. Differences on their team, with the company, with their key leaders. We are a business of people. People are all different because we all process and think about things differently. One of the most challenging things we will encounter is serving through differences and adversity. I mentioned my service mission for my church. Maybe you have seen young men in white shirts and ties around your area. That was me in my twenties! It wasn't easy to serve when people hated us. They had their own thoughts about religion, God, and us as missionaries. Sometimes people for whatever reasons from any walk of life outright hate us! Even people that are on our team or in our companies. On my mission, I wasn't there to serve only the people that accepted me. Our job was to serve and love everyone! So, think about your team right now. Have you cut off someone because there were struggles and differences? YOU get to decide what is best for you, but I want you to ask yourself why. Why were you not willing to serve someone?

Servant leadership can be lonely, and it can be hard to be the bigger person. Too many great leaders are lost to differences that get in the way. At this phase of leadership, I want to challenge every single one of you to take your personal development to the next level. You should be learning at this phase how to be a master of conflict resolution. As a servant leader, sometimes we have to serve through very rocky times. Uncertainty within the company comes up, arguments arise, and people can be downright aggressive and mean. There is training for this. There is no need to feel helpless and disengage because conflict arose. Your job as a servant leader is to train yourself on conflict resolution. I am going to give you five steps to start you on your conflict resolution training. If you want to learn more about this, I suggest coming to one of our Leader of Leaders Masterminds where I dive into this in more detail.

Here are five steps that I walk some of my leaders through when conflict arises in their business:

1 - Get the facts. There is a HUGE difference between facts and thoughts. Figure out the facts of the situation. Keep it factual and neutral.

2 - Identify both parties' thoughts about the facts. What are they thinking? This is usually where the conflict is happening. Listen from a place of neutrality and don't try to solve anything at this time. You are simply hearing what someone else is thinking. Great tip—ask open-ended questions.

3 - Gather the facts and thoughts and give yourself and everyone else involved time to think about it. Get coaching on your own thoughts about it, and really start to get into the shoes of everyone that is involved. See their side of it.

4 - Come up with solutions. Start to make a big list of all the solutions to what is going on. Don't filter any solutions out right now. Let everything be an option.

5 - Come together and validate that you have heard and understand all parties involved. Ask if they are willing to come discuss solutions and move forward. Come up with a solution and have all parties agree to move forward.

Now this is a very simple version of conflict resolution, but these simple steps have saved teams from falling apart. It has helped big companies work on tough problems, and it has even helped a husband and wife that had built a network marketing business together stay married. Simple steps work!

Every single cause that I have seen has had an opposite cause going against it. Even something that you think all of us could agree upon like ending child sex trafficking can't be agreed upon. You would think everyone would say YES, let's end this, but there is a HUGE market for it, and so it continues. The reason I bring this up is that it doesn't stop people from doing their best to end it. It makes an impact every single time an organization is taken down that has been promoting this. So, you have differences or outright hate toward someone on your team. Who are you NOT serving when you let that get in your way? Servant leaders are servants to all. They step up, dim the ego, work on conflict resolution, and serve their people. It doesn't mean that every single time they will take you up on your offer to serve, but you can still offer.

# YOUR JOB IS TO HOLD THE LINE

One thing I want to mention here that some people get confused. Servant leaders have strong boundaries! Yes, we love and serve everyone. But we do it in a way that makes sense and doesn't come from pleasing people. I am in servant leadership in my business, and I have rock-solid boundaries. You can't come to my house for a pop in. I won't answer the late-night messages, and I certainly don't let my business interrupt family time. These are boundaries I have put into place. Firm boundaries are always set from a place of love, but they are never to be crossed. Our job in this phase of leadership is to set boundaries and hold the line when and if anyone crosses them from a place of love. My team knows that if they cross the boundary, I will remind them and that we will work together within the boundaries that I set.

As Legacy leaders, we all understand how to show up and maintain firm boundaries. My job is not to get angry or upset when someone crosses the line. My job is to hold the line from a place of love, and never let anyone or anything disrupt that line. Same thing for you. As you show up in servant leadership for your team, company, leaders, etc., you will need to have rock-solid boundaries in place. Servant leaders know what to say yes to and what to say no to. They also understand that both "yes and no" are needed to maintain their house of order.

## What you can do right now to work on being a servant leader:

- Shift into helping others go after their dreams and create the success that they want in their lives.

- Get your own house in order so you can fully focus on helping other people. Go through the checklist and work on the areas of your life that you can see are lacking.

- Work on getting rid of an unhealthy ego and nurturing the healthy ego. Work on your self-confidence and knowing that it is great to love and be proud of yourself.

- Get training and develop the skills of conflict resolution.

- Create and stick to firm boundaries with your team.

*"If you're going to live, leave a legacy. Make a mark on the world that can't be erased."*

*— Maya Angelou*

CHAPTER 18

# THE LIVING
# LEGACY LEADER

Ancient Greece is known as one of the most iconic influences in the developed Western civilizations. Many things that were created back then still thrive in this day almost unchanged. From politics, literature, and sports, there are very few areas that Ancient Greece didn't leave a mark on. So how did ancient Greece leave such a lasting legacy?

First, they were innovators and allowed people to think and explore. They rewarded thinking outside of the box. Second, the people were willing to adjust and adapt. As they played around with their own language, the people of Greece were adaptable. They created systems and were always tweaking to see how to make it better. Like their water system. Someone came up with a complex system, and several people started using it, playing around with it. They weren't fixated on who did what, they were more interested in the outcome. Third, they welcomed debate, criticism, and different opinions. They saw this as part of their jobs to not only listen but be willing to decide for themselves in the end what they thought was best. That is how we create a lasting legacy.

We have so many things documented about ancient Greece because of inventions. The ancient Greek invention of the alphabet made it possible to write and categorize. Phonetic letters made literacy accessible to anyone capable of learning the sounds of oral vocabulary. The Olympics serve as one of ancient Greece's most visible legacies, dating from 776 BC. Named for their location at Olympia, the site of the original games, the ancient Greek Olympics have persisted for almost 1,200 years. The modern marathon also stands as a legacy of Greek athletic achievement. The ancient Greeks forged a strong legacy in politics, most notable through the invention of democracy.

The accomplishments and legacy left by ancient Greece is far-reaching. So how do we all create a lasting legacy? This is where your passion, vision, culture, etc., all come into play. Legacy cannot be created without the foundation that you have created throughout your business in network marketing. The phases of leadership are all built upon one another. Legacy leadership is the top of the pyramid. It is the pinnacle of the phases of leadership because it can't be built without everything coming before it.

# LIVING IN YOUR LEGACY

Leading with a legacy mindset is doing a lot of things like Stephen Covey talks about. As a legacy leader, you are beginning with the end in mind. Legacy leaders are crystal clear on what type of legacy they want to leave. They create with purpose and with their legacy in mind. For me, I have always said that my legacy is being able to leave loved ones with memories, not dreams of what could have been.

Taking our kids on these vacations isn't just about traveling. It is a dream builder exercise. It's a way to have the time to have conversations and experiences that we may not have had if we stayed home. It's a way to be able to create those lifelong memories. So, we've already at this point in life and have done the 12-year-old trip with our two oldest children. I already talked about the epic trip that my oldest and I were able to go on. As time has passed, I am starting to see how the memories of the trip with my oldest son are shaping the type of man he is becoming. I told you all that it was the memories that were created that I was most proud of. But to be honest, it is watching the man he is becoming that makes me the proudest. I see that directly correlated to the memories, conversations, and experiences we had while we were on that trip.

One of the things that helped me get to the next level in business is really wanting to create a legacy. Having the bigger picture, bigger concepts, and bigger principles have always driven me in my own life. This is what I see at play for legacy leaders as well. At our seven-figure masterminds, we talk a lot about legacy leadership. I am always blown away by people that are driving their business with legacy leadership. I spoke with one woman that is building homes and helping girls' schools in Africa. She has her whole team and community that takes part in helping this happen. It is awesome to see her legacy leadership impact places all over the world. I also see many of my seven and eight-figure earners start nonprofits, serve their communities, and even create history in their part of the world. All these people are leading with legacy. They know what they are trying to create and what they want to be known for. They go out and intentionally run their lives and businesses around this legacy.

My wife and I began our marriage with legacy in mind. We have set goals around becoming the type of grandparents that we want to be. This happened before we even had kids! We began with that legacy in mind.

Even my business and what I create is about legacy. I write books and so much content on social media because I know that content will live on. It will be here even after I am gone. I can make an impact and perhaps be an influence to my grandchildren and great-grandchildren. This is legacy leadership. It is the next level of leadership. Not only do you want to have that legacy-type vision and mindset. You also want to be able to transfer that into other people's guts and mindsets and help them to be able to dream bigger and think bigger and think with having that legacy in mind.

This past year I have spent countless hours focusing on the legacy I want to create with my business. I have created a lot so far, but the vision, mission, and values of my company are so much greater. I want to create a legacy that impacts the entire network marketing industry and helps every single person make money in network marketing. To do this, I have to step outside of my comfort zone and go all in on becoming a living legacy leader in this industry.

# PREPARE FOR IMPACT

Legacy leaders focus on impact. You have to start spending your time in the places where you will have the most impact. I did a mastermind with the top leaders in the industry, and I took a poll. I asked them, "How many of you have spoken on a stage with hundreds of people in the room?" Every single hand went up. "How many of you have spoken to thousands?" Again, every single hand. "How many of you have strategically figured out the top 5 percent of people on your team and dedicated hours to their development?" Only a couple of hands went up.

Leadership isn't always about being on the stage. Yes, it's fun. Yes, it's a milestone for every single person in network marketing. But, in the legacy phase of leadership, we are focusing on shifting from the masses, spending our time with everyone, to spending 95 percent of our time with the top five percent of people in your business. YES, you read that right. You should be spending 95 percent of your time with only five percent of people in your business.

Legacy leaders are starting to have their own masterminds and retreats. They are focusing on making sure that they get their top five percent to THEIR next level of leadership. I have a good friend and client that has been coming to my retreats religiously for years. She is moving into legacy leadership and is starting to host her own high-level retreats for her team. She is investing in the five percent.

It doesn't always have to be retreats. Each person is going to find their own legacy path that will serve and have the highest impact. It could be retreats, books, podcasts, nonprofit organizations that you start working with. I have another leader that has started her own nonprofit. She organizes and includes her charity work as part of the culture of people that she brings into her team. Her company does company trips that people can earn, but her personal team does nonprofit trips where the top five percent can earn a trip to serve the community and come and get extra training from her. Turns out her team trips are far more coveted than the company trips!

Legacy leaders are focused on making the highest impact in their businesses, communities, and homes. Because ultimately, they know that having the highest impact in these areas is what will make the most impact in the world.

Legacy leaders have to reevaluate their purpose, mission, vision, and values. At the last mastermind I hosted, we were talking about how to crush their business in this phase. Someone said, "Rob, I have an honest question that I need you to answer. WHY? Why would I want to crush my business? I have everything I want. I make more money than I ever thought possible. What's the point of crushing anything?"

That, my friends, is why you must reevaluate your purpose, vision, and values at this stage of leadership. We talked about this before, but you have already created the lifestyle phase of your life. Most people get burnt out here and retire. You are making enough money and think that the easy street is now where you are strolling. You have got to go find something bigger than network marketing. Yes, you heard me correctly. You have to find the thing OUTSIDE of network marketing that will drive you INSIDE network marketing.

Let me give you some examples. My friend that started her nonprofit told me that she would never be as driven in her business if she didn't have an entire village school in Africa relying on her. She is driven IN her business by her passion OUTSIDE of network marketing.

I have a client that started a podcast that has nothing to do with network marketing. She loves doing a weekly podcast about the subject. But it is her business that gives her the freedom to create the podcast. Her passion OUTSIDE network marketing is funded by what she does INSIDE her business.

Finding the passion and drive outside has given several of my clients the drive to once again find the passion and drive in network marketing. It doesn't matter if you are brand new, or the highest-paid person in your company. If your why isn't solid you will get burnt out and quit working. It is the very same thing for legacy leaders. You will find more energy and passion for your business if you find a WHY outside of network marketing.

Recently I hosted a ten-day mastermind. For the first half of the mastermind, I had legacy leaders attend. For the second half of the time, I hosted the mastermind for some of the up-and-coming leaders in network marketing. It was fascinating to see the different types of conversations and questions that were being asked at both masterminds. Neither was better than the other, but there was a big difference. Here are a couple of my observations. First, legacy leaders don't have HOW greed. They don't come worrying about how to do everything. They come to listen and soak it all in. They come knowing that they can figure it out. They come knowing they will be successful in whatever they put their minds to. Second, the legacy leaders talked about their team rather than themselves.

# BE WHERE YOUR FEET ARE PLANTED

The other day I heard someone say, "Be where your feet are planted." At first, I thought to myself, "You are always where your feet are planted!" But then I looked around. I was in public with my family, and as I looked around, I realized that there were only two people that weren't looking down at their phones. Every other person in this very crowded area had their head down. No one was actually where their feet were planted. They were off in the online space.

I love social media and doing business online. It is fantastic and has helped many of us build very successful businesses. As we work on being a legacy leader, we need to be more intentional with being where our feet are planted. People look forward to being around you, speaking with you, getting pictures with you, and hearing your words of wisdom. If you are completely disconnected from what is around you, you may miss an opportunity to make an impact with the person that is right in front of you.

I have a friend that is a huge leader in her industry. She has made a commitment to never be on social media when she is out in public. She may take pictures or videos, but she never posts them right away.

When I asked her about this, she told me that she never wanted to be engaged online and miss in-person meetups with those around her. She said, "It's great that we have the online option, but how much better are in-person events?! It's the same when meeting people. I can connect online, but if someone is right in front of me, it is going to be a bigger impact seeing them face to face." Be where your feet are planted. Sometimes my wife teases me when I am hosting an event, and everyone wants to talk with me. She says, "You are kind of a big deal." In the legacy leadership phase, we are a big deal! People want to be around us, so give them an opportunity to do that.

Be where you are. Look people in the eyes. Really listen to what they are saying. Then be willing to impact their lives by sharing. I remember being at church once. There was a successful businessman in my church whom I always respected. One day I was struggling with something in my business, and I happened to mention it to this man at church while we sat next to each other. The man turned to me, looked me in the eyes, and then asked a couple of questions. He said, "Why do you think you are struggling with that in particular right now?" and then asked, "What are some solutions that you can come up with?" He listened intently the entire time I was answering. He then sat for a moment thinking and gave me a very thoughtful response. I felt seen, validated, and he also made me feel like I was absolutely going to figure this out. THAT is what legacy leadership looks like in action.

Being a living legacy is not easy. Where much is given, much is required. Throughout this whole book, I have been giving you the blueprint so that you can reach this level of leadership. Don't toss it away or think that it isn't a big deal. It is! As hard as you have worked to get here, your job isn't close to being complete. As legacy leaders, it is our responsibility to show others how to do the same. This can all be done while maintaining strong boundaries and showing up how it feels best for you.

# DON'T FIZZLE OUT

After retirement, Kobe Bryant didn't stop leading. He was a mentor to many up-and-coming stars. He also took a special interest in the WNBA and started to be an advocate for women's sports. Kobe didn't decide to be done with leadership when he retired. He moved into the legacy phase of leadership and continued to lead from the front in places he was passionate about. Even after his tragic passing, Kobe continues to have a leadership role in the communities in which he was serving. One of the reasons that Kobe's legacy lives on was his passionate commitment to things that matter to him.

It is crucial in this phase of leadership that you are finding your passion in mentorship and going all in on it. What are you extremely passionate about? What could you spend hours talking about? What lights you up in your life? One of the biggest struggles I see in this phase of leadership is something I call "fizzle out." It is a cousin to burnout. We talked about burnout in previous chapters and how it can impact you and your business. "Fizzle out" is when someone in the legacy phase of leadership feels like there is nothing else to do. They start to tell themselves that they have nothing to offer and that everything that can be done has been done. They have reached all the ranks, everyone they have mentored can do it on their own, they have won all the trips and made all the money they have ever wanted to have in their life. They aren't burnt out from anything; they simply are ready to "fizzle out."

The "fizzle out" is caused by losing passion. As you progress in leadership, you must be willing to continue to find your passion. It doesn't matter if your passions are in network marketing, or outside of it, but you must continue to work on the vision and passions of your life. I told you the story of the woman helping single moms in her community. That is her passion. The driver behind that passion is her business. I have another legacy leader that has a passion for launching new builders. They have made it their life's work to launch thousands of people's network marketing businesses. BOTH of these examples of legacy leaders are people driven by passion. What can you do if you notice that you are close to "fizzling out"? Here are my five tips to avoid "fizzle out":

1 - Travel. Get out of your own space and travel somewhere. Doesn't matter if it is to a local hotel or an international trip. Get out and spend some time traveling. This is one of the major things in my life that helps me remember and identify things that I am passionate about.

2 - Re-evaluate your life. Sometimes in the "fizzle out" phase, we forget that we have choices that we are making every single day, and that we could choose something different for ourselves at any time. Spend some time going through your choices and then intentionally choose what you want!

3 - Only do what lights you up and hire out for the rest! At this phase of leadership, you should be able to afford whatever help you want. Don't be doing things that don't light you up. If you love one step in a five-step process, hire everything else out.

4 - Look at leveling up your network. There are people out there doing bigger and better things than you are right now. Anytime I find a leader stuck thinking that they have done "all the things" I have them start networking at different events. This usually gets them out of their own circle and see what else can be accomplished. Get out and find people that light a fire under you.